The First 649 Days

Praise for *The First 649 Days*

"Eric LeMay's *The First 649 Days* is a tender, devastating series of reports from the early years of a cancer diagnoses, a global pandemic, and parenthood. 'I was / with / my absence,' LeMay writes as he accounts for each day or moment's details, accumulating urgently toward a life's tableau. *The First 649 Days* is a largehearted exploration of love's capacities as well as an experiment in documenting the now via forms as various as a cancer diary, children's book, birth story, field guide, afterworld address, medical erasures, first words journal, pandemic triptych, birdseed performance piece, and worry list, among others. Throughout this gorgeous amassing of ordinary days in anything-but-ordinary circumstances, the reader might find themselves wondering if the form of the essay is still our finest technology for keeping memory alive. LeMay confirms: 'It's what I have,' and then he gives it to us."—**Caryl Pagel,** author of *Out of Nowhere Into Nothing*

"Eric LeMay's *The First 649 Days* is a work of breathtaking honesty and heart. LeMay captures life's singular moments—the birth of a child, unexpected illness, mortality—exquisitely, revealing the precarious beauty of our world through the eyes of his young son Ro. LeMay's inventive renderings are a brilliant reminder that our lives may harbor threat, disappointment, and grief, yet still shimmer with hope and wild beauty at every turn."

—**Dinty W. Moore**, author of *Between Panic & Desire*

"*The First 649 Days* is worth its weight in gold, mined responsibly from the veins of Eric LeMay's heart. In its shine you may find yours. Perhaps you'll meet the parent you want to be or give voice to your silenced inner Hamlet. You may awaken with him at Fox Lake to the body's vulnerability or warm with gratitude for those nurses who can gentle terror. Certainly, this private reckoning invites communion, as the birds commune over feasts of seeds he presents as poetry on paper altars. *How do you want to be remembered?* we ask alongside him and, for his considerations, answer wiser."

—**Amy Wright,** author of *Paper Concert: A Conversation in the Round*

"How to describe a book as so profoundly human as *The First 649 Days?* LeMay's archive of parenthood during a global pandemic reckons with many of life's heavier subjects—illness and mortality, anxiety about the future, the ever-present threat of gun violence—woven into the fabric of the small moments that, taken together, comprise the whole of our lives: bringing a newborn baby home, long walks in the Appalachian wilds, conversations over spoonfuls of sherbet. The essays in *The First 649 Days* are a celebration of love and its resilience in the face of unthinkable circumstances and a resonant contemporary record of our time."—**Zoë Bossiere,** author of *Cactus Country: A Boyhood Memoir*

Praise for Eric LeMay

"Eric LeMay's *Immortal Milk* does for cheese all that ought to be done for cheese: it takes something micro, the history of milk gone bad, and turns it into something macro, the story of how the way we eat becomes the way we live."—**Adam Gopnik,** author of *Paris to the Moon*

"The next best thing to tasting the cheese itself . . . a warm, even gooey, appreciation of a much-loved and often misunderstood food."

—***Publisher's Weekly***

"Clearly, this is someone who not only celebrates cheese, but also the written word, which is what makes *Immortal Milk* such a great read."

—**Domenica Marchetti,** *The Washington Post*

"A lively collection of pensées, LeMay's *In Praise of Nothing* is a charming investigation of memory, humor, serendipity, and the existential problem of 'being me.'"—**Christina Thompson,** author of *Come on Shore and We Will Kill and Eat You All*

"Eric LeMay writes of his Ohio upbringing—watching Boy George on TV, mythologizing Patient Zero during the AIDS pandemic, receiving (and rebelling against) communiqués from his father via Post-Its—with a rare and welcome quietude. Nothing in this book feels amped-up or overblown. I love it."—**John Bresland,** author of *Zero Station and Other Essays*

The First 649 Days

Essays and Other Acts of Love

Eric LeMay

The Kent State University Press *Kent, Ohio*

ISBN 978-1-60635-506-0 (paperback)
ISBN 978-1-63101-584-7 (epub)
Published in the United States of America

Cataloging information for this title is available at the Library of Congress.

Contents

Ohio Ground

From my kitchen window, I can see the grove of white pines where I'd like to be buried.

Washing lettuce or dirty plates, I'll look up and see them. Across the field, their bristly green tops rise like the prow of a great ship cresting a wave. In storms, their branches pulse. Occasionally, the shadow of a turkey vulture or red-tailed hawk flashes across them and draws my eyes skyward. In the evening, they're the last trees to catch the sunset. Pinkish-orange light climbs their tips until, at last, they become shadows. I watch them as the faucet runs.

My burial spot is where several trees have fallen. Their trunks crisscross one another. Their wood is soft and spongy, full of pin-sized holes where bark beetles have made their homes. Waxy ferns spring from them. Tufts of moss pock them. In summer, grasshoppers, damselflies, and mosquitos hover and buzz. The spot looks very much alive.

This is where I'd like to be buried, my bones among these bones of pine.

*

For most of my life, I haven't much thought about being buried.

I remember once as a child going to my uncle's funeral with my grandmother. Afterward, she said she wanted to visit her cemetery plot. She led me to a nearby marble headstone. Inscribed on one side were my grandfather's name and dates. On the other, a smooth gray surface waited for hers.

“There it is,” she said and stared down through grass.

I remember looking away. Old farmhouses lined the street. Beyond them began fields that led to more farms and more fields. This was Covington, Ohio, deforested flatlands not far from the Indiana border. My grandparents grew up on family farms, where death and life are as plain as the land. Cemeteries mark the outskirts of towns, the way churches mark their centers.

I also remember the gravediggers under a far tree, waiting for us to leave.

*

2 A few years later, I made a trip with my father to Waynesville, Ohio, the town where he’d grown up. We stopped by the family plot.

I remember his excitement as he pointed out different relatives, as well as the places where he, my mother, and his sister would be buried. I took it in. These were the LeMays, graves with my name on them. At some point, my father noticed something I had also noticed: There wasn’t a plot for me. His mood flagged, then he half-laughed.

“I guess we’ll have to see if there are other spots available.” He shrugged and walked off.

I looked around. The cemetery was already overcrowded with graves. I did see a newish area in the distance, one much less scenic. Did I want to be buried in an annex? I didn’t see much point to being buried in the family cemetery if I wasn’t going to be buried with my family.

*

Once I had the chance, I left Ohio.

At various times, I lived in Philadelphia and New York, outside of Chicago, Washington DC, and Boston. I felt at home in cities, where I could hear other languages, look up at skyscrapers, browse bookstores. Home, for me, wasn't a specific place so much as the life that urban places made possible.

And books were essential to it. I remember one evening when a Jewish friend said, offhandedly, in his thick Slavic accent, "Oh, Eric, you have no home. You are a people of the book."

That felt right. I was a people of the book, secular for sure, but no less devoted to words as a way of life. And I lived that life for decades. Books were where I found my people, not only the living but also the dead, those whose writing became a kind of afterlife.

Even now, I sometimes feel as though I'm burying myself in the books I write, perhaps none more so than this one.

*

And yet, Ohio has always marked me.

For college, I crossed the state, where I discovered a wholly different land: The foothills of the Appalachian Mountains, with their thick forests that went on for miles and their rugged sandstone outcroppings. I watched as deer plodded nonchalantly through the brick streets of my town and redwing blackbirds flited along the reedy banks of the Hocking River.

I fell in love with this Ohio, with the feeling of being nooked in by the hills, with its winter skies and wildflowers.

So when I had the chance to move back, almost twenty years later, I did. I'd recently gotten married, and my wife, Kristin, and I decided to leave New York. Before long, we couldn't imagine going back. We could, however, imagine a child, one growing up in the woods outside our door, with a creek not far off. And then we had one.

We named him Roland, which quickly became "Ro."

*

In that creek near us, the water pools bright red and orange. The colors come from acid runoff, from the coal mines that started here centuries ago.

The creek itself is named Margaret Creek, after the first white woman to settle in this place. Surely, the people who lived here before her—the Shawnee, Osage, Mingo, Erie, Lenape, Wyandot, and Miami—knew it by other names.

It's also the creek where Ro learned to skip stones. He started with what we called "kerplunks," because that's the sound the stones made before he could skip them. Over months, he worked at it: how to cock his arm, how to flick the stone. And then one day, it happened. His stone skipped across the water, skip-skip-skip, rippling outward in rings.

This is the place of Ro's childhood, where his feet first touched the grass. And this is the place where, with luck, he'll bury me. In a grove of white pines. Maybe the wind stirs the high branches. Maybe a crow caws. Maybe the light filters down.

Birth Story

In the snow dark of an Appalachian winter, we brought Ro home.

It's been days now, and none of us has really slept. Night slips into dawn, dawn into day, the sun sets or maybe never rises. We hardly notice.

Gray clouds lacquer the sky and hang over the matted field and leafless woods. Crows shuttle back and forth. Everything beyond the trees feels far off, unreal, as if Ro has drawn us back into a womb of sorts, one enclosed by cold and silence and ice.

We huddle together. We hunker down. We wait.

*

Ro wasn't ready to be born. None of us are. By our very nature we enter the world too soon because, as humans, we must. Our brains force us to. Over millions of years, we've evolved in such a way that we aren't born when we should be. Our brains are too large, and large brains mean large heads, and large heads can't pass from the womb through the pelvis into the world.

If we're going to be born at all, we have to be born early, before we've fully developed. Nine months isn't enough. We're not done gestating. Ideally, we'd have another three months in the womb. Ideally, we'd have what's often called a fourth trimester.

That's why Kristin and I, as best we can, have been trying to recreate Ro's life in the womb. We feed him as soon as he needs feeding. We wear him in slings and carriers, so he can feel the warmth and movement of our bodies. We swaddle him, so he can sleep. We keep him close and cared for.

We also fill our bedroom with noise. White noise. The womb isn't a quiet place. Babies hear the thrumming of their heartbeat and the larger heart above them. They hear the swishing of blood through veins and the gurgle of stomach acid. Far off, through the muffle of amniotic fluid, as in a dream, they also hear the world: clanking pots, car horns, and, of course, the voice of the person they inhabit, the first voice they'll recognize when they're finally born.

What babies can't hear when they're in the womb—can't because they can't—is their own cries.

*

Kristin and I first heard Ro's cry in the operating room.

Kristin went through five days of strong contractions and no sleep, followed by sixteen hours of labor, first at home, then at the hospital. At hour seventeen, the baby's heartrate started decelerating during her contractions. This meant our baby might not be getting oxygen.

After reading the heart monitor, our midwife knelt and spoke to us.

"It would be medical malpractice to let you labor any longer," she said. "I'm recommending an emergency C-section."

And so, in minutes, we found ourselves under the bright lights of the operating room, with Kristin strapped to a stainless-steel table, a curtain draped across her chest, and me in ill-fitting scrubs, standing beside her.

We'd hoped for a natural birth, for much the same reason we now live with white noise: A baby makes a hard transition from the womb to the world, so we wanted to make that moment as easy, as comforting, as noninvasive as possible. A slide through the birth canal and onto Kristin's breast.

Instead, there we were, behind a flimsy curtain, listening to the surgeon's directions, listening for that moment when we'd hear that everything was all right, that our baby was healthy, was alive. We were listening for our baby's cry.

And after a short forever, we heard it: loud and powerful and, to our ears, glorious. We heard it and heard it.

The nurses didn't bring Ro to us right away. Instead, from behind the curtain, we heard the scuttle and bustle of tests and measurements. "Place him here . . . Check his flexion . . ."

I should say that, in addition to not wanting a surgical birth, we also hadn't wanted to know our baby's gender. We found that out when the nurses started using pronouns for a baby behind a curtain we had yet to see. At some point, amid all the tests, one of the nurses whispered, "I don't think they know yet."

From then on, as we waited and waited, the nurses tried to keep us guessing. "Place him there," they'd say, "or *her.*" "Get his diaper," they'd say. "Or *hers.*" One of the residents finally brought Ro around the curtain, his tiny body veiled in an oversized yellow diaper.

"Would you like to see your baby?" she asked.

We would, we did.

With a flourish, she removed the diaper and unveiled Ro's penis. He cried and cried. Right up until the nurse held him against Kristin's face, and he heard her voice. Then he stopped.

*

I'd like to leave it at that. I'd like to say that, after such a rough entry into the world, Ro recovered in Kristin's arms. But that didn't happen.

Due to other complications during the labor, there was a risk that Ro might have a blood infection. Maybe sepsis. Maybe meningitis. So, not long after Kristin finally got to hold and feed him, two phlebotomists in bright red scrubs came into our room and explained that Ro needed blood tests. They needed to take him to the lab.

At this point, Kristin also isn't doing well: She's hemorrhaging large amounts of blood. Her uterus isn't contracting as quickly as it should, not returning to its normal shape. Our nurse is looking more and more grave.

She and I talk and decide I should go with Ro.

I follow the phlebotomists down a long empty hallway. It's night now, maybe 9:00 pm, and very still. When we reach the lab, I'm asked to stay outside. I watch the scene unfold through one of those windows with reinforced wire that crisscrosses the glass. It's like looking into a police precinct or a prison. I watch as the phlebotomists unwrap Ro and search his legs and arms for a vein. He's crying again, shrieking, and pulling against them. Finally, one of the phlebotomists sticks him with a needle. She shakes her head. No luck. She sticks him again. He keeps screaming. And again. Nope. Nope. And then, finally, she hits a viable spot. She puts in the hep-lock and starts drawing blood.

I watch as they fill vials. Ro is still screaming. They're holding him down. Finally, after three or four different vials, they remove the hep-lock and start wrapping him in a blanket. Ro hasn't stopped crying. At least it's over.

*

Except I see one of the phlebotomists staring at a vial against the light, giving it a little shake, then a bigger shake. Finally, it's her head that shakes. She looks at me and makes her way over to the lab door. As it opens, I feel sick.

"We have to do it again," she says. "It didn't work—he has such little veins."

I nod. Okay. If he has a blood infection, his life is in danger and he needs to start treatment for it. And there's no other way to find out. I watch the entire scene unfold again. The sticking, the blood, Ro's struggles and screams. And again, it ends with her shaking her head. No, she couldn't get enough blood. No, it didn't work.

"We're going to let the morning shift try," she says.

I take Ro back down the long hall.

"Where have you been?" asks Kristin.

I explain what happened, trying to minimize how bad it was. She looks ghostly. She doesn't have enough blood in her body. I figure she doesn't need to worry about something we can't change. I hand her Ro, and he nuzzles into her. Maybe he sleeps, maybe he feeds. I can't remember.

*

What I do remember is our nurse coming back in to check on Kristin's bleeding.

The nurse pulls up the sheets, and I see what Kristin can't: a thick pool of blood. I help the nurse change the pads beneath her, and at some point, another nurse enters. She explains that Ro needs to do the blood tests again. Right now. The pediatrician on call has said it's crucial. It can't wait until morning.

I explain to this second nurse, as politely as I can, that Ro has already been through the procedure twice and that the two phlebotomists strike me as well-meaning fuckups. I'm not going to let them try it again.

Oh no, the nurse explains, she's going to do it herself this time, not the phlebotomists. "And I'm really good at it," she says. The other nurse nods, "Yep, she is."

Then why, I ask myself, *didn't you do it from the start?*

Off I go again, taking Ro back to the lab, once again leaving Kristin.

The scene is basically the same. I'm behind the same wired glass, looking in, only now Ro is under a heat lamp, like a sad cafeteria meal. This new nurse—her name is Joy—takes Ro through the same process: the needle, the vials, the cries and shrieks. And she succeeds, in part because she literally milks Ro's flesh, squeezing and pumping it to get more blood. She also recruits a second nurse. It takes two of them to pin down Ro's arm and stick in the needle.

But finally, he's free.

I take him back down the long hallway, back to Kristin. She's starting to do better. Her bleeding has slowed, though her skin is the dull color of thrift-store lace.

A few hours tick by, maybe two. Ro collapses into a soundless sleep. My parents visit. Kristin sleeps. Things, it seems, are settling.

*

Then, in comes Joy.

The initial blood tests don't look good. Ro is going to need six courses of antibiotics in the next forty-eight hours. We can choose: They can give him six rounds of shots, or he can have it all through an IV, but if we use the IV, he'll have to keep the needle in his arm constantly, so the vein doesn't close.

We choose the IV.

And it's back down the hallway with Ro.

"I figured this would happen," says Joy, "so I saved a good vein in his hand."

I don't know if I'm supposed to be impressed? Appreciative? Furious, because she didn't use the good vein earlier and make it easier on him? I'm not sure, and, anyway, I'm so overwhelmed that whatever I say will be wrong. I think I just say, "Thanks."

Back under the heat lamp, one more big needle stick, and then Joy attaches the IV, which she secures by wrapping up Ro's arm in what looks like a massive cast. It's about the size of his thigh and it will keep him from using his arm for the next forty-eight hours, the first two days of his life.

At the end of those two days, the pediatrician comes into our room. She informs us there's no blood infection. All those alarming markers that all those tests found, they were result of the natural stresses that Ro experienced in labor. No sepsis poisoning him, no meningitis swelling the lining of his brain. He's fine. Just fine.

And we're grateful, of course. Thank you, doctor, thank you.

We also realize—we look at each other, even as she's telling us—that all those trips down the hallway, all that time away from Kristin as she was hemorrhaging and alone, all those times Ro cried out for her and against the needles and the abuse, all of that was for nothing.

*

So here we are, days later, still in the white noise of the womb: heartbeat after heartbeat. It plays from a small speaker on the bedstand. We hear it in the day, when Ro naps, and in the night, if and when he sleeps.

Outside, a new snow covers the hillside.

Ro's fourth trimester won't end for months, when winter turns toward spring and when, I suppose, he'll experience a new birth of sorts. We're hoping for something better, for him and for us, but we don't know what.

Right now, we hold him close, all of us wrapped together in this makeshift womb, and wonder what's on the other side.

Mapa

From the start, I failed at being a dad. I failed on the night Ro was born, and I failed in the days that followed. I tried. I'd have these moments where I'd say to myself, *I'm a dad now. What's a dad?* And then these dad clichйs would swarm me. Dads are supportive. Dads are warm. Dads are protective, knowing, and capable. Dads teach you how to change a flat tire, throw a punch, shave. That's a dad. I wondered if I should buy a ball cap.

At the hospital, as a new dad with a newborn, I hovered over the nurses, offering to help. They let me know the best way I could help was by getting out of their way. They were the pros. They knew how to take care of mom and baby, thank you very much. I didn't. Moreover, in their narrowing eyes, I sensed a general distrust of dad, that dad would not only *not* help, but also botch things. I sensed everyone in the natal unit would be better off, including dad, if dad weren't around.

My own dad confirmed my feeling when he visited the hospital. After he and my mother had met Ro and were getting ready to leave, he told me he'd reserved their hotel room for an extra day. Would I like to use it to get some sleep? I looked at Kristin, recovering from a C-section, and Ro, only a day old, and told him absolutely no way was I going anywhere. He looked hurt. After all, he was just following dad logic: Baby is fine; mom is fine; nurses are here to look after baby and mom; and there's a nice hotel room, for free. Why not use it?

Later, I learned that's what he did when I was born. After my mother gave birth, I had to stay in the nursery for almost a week. My mother had had a bad reaction to a spinal tap and needed to stay prone. My dad would visit the hospital every day after work. He'd sit with my mom, then he'd go to the nursery viewing window. (Dads weren't allowed in the nursery.) He'd see if he could spot me among all the infants lined up in the plastic bassinets. He'd tap on the glass and wave. Then he'd leave. What else was dad supposed to do?

When he told me this story, about a year after Ro was born, I asked him what stood out to him most. I was imagining how hard it must have been not to hold your baby in those first days. I also imagined how hard it must have been for me, as a baby, not to be held. I'd basically been handed over at birth to a few nurses and left for a week in a plastic tub. My dad thought about it, then he brightened and said that, because my mom wasn't home, he got to go out to eat a lot.

And that, I suppose, is what dads did. They got out of the way. They got some sleep. They ate burgers at White Castle while nurses did or didn't watch over their wives and newborn children. I couldn't do that. After Ro was born, I stayed at the hospital. I slept in the same room as he and Kristin on a foldout pleather recliner. I ate cold burritos in the middle of the night that friends had brought because there was too much to do in the middle of the day to eat. I did this because I wanted to be there. I wanted to bounce our baby, swaddle our baby, coo and cuddle our baby. I wanted to check and double-check that our baby was still breathing. I wanted to do what I could, so Kristin could heal, so Ro could sense that he was cared for and loved. What I didn't do, what I couldn't do, was dad.

Maybe I could mom? Once we brought Ro home, I supported Kristin by doing the work traditionally dumped on mom. I'd always done a lot of domestic labor, but now I tried to do it all. The dishes, the laundry, the cleaning, the trash. I got the groceries and picked up the takeout. I changed every dirty diaper and ordered new ones in bulk. I took Ro on long walks, so Kristin could shower or nap. I held Ro so she could pee. It was exhausting. I was running on old coffee and living in old clothes. I bathed, when I had the chance, with baby wipes. I smelled like antiseptic and stress.

I was also working full time, which I suppose means I wasn't only a mom but a supermom. We both were. Kristin was caring for an infant who needed her constantly. She was breastfeeding day and night, struggling to find moments to sleep between Ro's cries for, as she put it, "the boobs." And after her brief maternity leave ended, she also had to add her own work onto Ro's already overwhelming needs. I wasn't nearly the village of moms she needed, but I was better than momming alone. Ro always had one of us there to hold him and care for him. I wouldn't have traded that for hygiene.

To my surprise, the only people who didn't like me being mom were other moms. I'd take Ro to the library or community center for story hour or playtime, and the other moms would scowl at me, an obvious predator. I'd watch them tighten their circle and think, *But I have a baby, like you! I'm literally wearing a baby!* It didn't matter. I may have had a baby, but they had babies and lattes and leggings and maternal suspicions. I'd never be a mom among the moms.

Still, I tried. I'd overhear them talking about feeding schedules, sleep regressions, eczema, and car-seat safety and I knew that I could talk this talk. I, too, had lived through spit-ups, teething, and the impossible search for a reliable local pediatrician. Sometimes I'd say so. And sometimes it worked. The moms and I would get to talking and suddenly I'd be in the circle, connecting with them through our shared struggles as moms. Sometimes they'd forget I was there to eat their babies.

Once, I remember the moms started talking about breastfeeding. I was already in the circle and thought, *This could get weird. I don't want this to get weird.* I decided I'd just listen, listen and hope my silence felt supportive or, if not, made me invisible. Back and forth they went, talking about plugged ducts, milk flows, biting. I nodded and I winced. And it got weird. The moms were sharing their most intimate concerns about their babies and their bodies, and none of us could pretend I wasn't there and I wasn't me.

So I decided I'd chime in. I said, brightly, how the other day I was watching Kristin breastfeed and I noticed that Ro had these delicate blue veins spreading outward from the corner of his mouth through his whole body and how, under the skin of Kristin's nipple, I could see similar blue veins, also spreading outward from her breast through her body, and how I felt this sense of awe as I watched Kristin feeding Ro, literarily keeping him alive, through this network of vines that seemed to connect them as one being and how watching them reminded me of the tree of life, with its branches reaching up into the sky and its roots burrowing down into the ground and its trunk connecting the heavens and the earth, and that maybe, at that very moment, I was actually seeing life itself, life creating life, and learning what it truly means for us to care for one another as human beings, that we are, by our very natures, branches of one another, roots of one another, and I said all of this, brightly, to all the moms, who were now all staring at me because, as I said, I didn't want it to get weird.

No, I couldn't dad, and, no, I couldn't mom. I was out of options. At least that's what I thought, up until the time Ro began learning to talk. When he first started, he would sound out these basic syllables. *Ba ba. Ah ah.* But before long, those syllables stretched and rounded, and I thought, *Here comes his first word.* Kristin did, too, and she was determined Ro's first word would be *mama.* Not *mom,* but *mama.* Unlike me, she didn't want to be a mom. She scorned the clichŭs that made up mom: Moms drive minivans; moms wear mom shoes; moms grow mom butts. Not her. She'd be hip. She'd be mama.

To ensure this, she started repeating *mama* to Ro. *Mama, mama, mama, say it, say it, mama, say it, mama, mama, say it.* And before long, he did. *Mama* was Ro's first word. And from that moment on, I was destined to become *papa.* It wasn't Ro's next word. *Cat* came first. But before long, I was papa, and Kristin was mama, and our parental identities seemed set.

Until, that is, a few months later. For some reason, Ro suddenly stopped calling me *papa.* Instead, as though he'd never called me anything else, he started calling me *mapa.* Mapa? At first, I wasn't sure if he was making a mistake or if, as he was learning more and more words, he'd hit some cognitive overload and needed time to sort out all the language he was absorbing. Learning to talk isn't easy. But he kept calling me *mapa.* And as he did, I began to wonder who this mapa might be? A mix of mama and papa? An alternative to the two? *Mapa* certainly felt more like me than the alternatives. And it was so easy, so natural, even a child could say it. And did.

In fact, *mapa* would eventually lead me to a truer sense of who I am. Years later, I'd discover other words—*gender fluid, gender expansive, nonbinary, trans*—but *mapa* has always felt the truest. I'm not saying that Ro, at a little under a year old, had the miraculous ability to see my true gender. He soon went back to calling me *papa* and still does. What I'm saying is that, in his struggle to learn how to speak, he mashed together two syllables that, for him, momentarily seemed right. Suddenly, I became mapa. And, for me, *mapa* also seemed right. It made the invisible visible. It showed me a truth about myself I'd never seen and maybe never would have seen had Ro not said it. *Mapa.* What a gift.

I think about the night Ro was born. I was the first one to hold him, really hold him. Kristin had undergone a C-section and had to stay in the operating room. The nurses took me aside and asked me to wheel Ro in this little plastic cart down to our room. When we got there, Ro was squirming and crying and new to the world, so I did what any mapa would do: I peeled off my shirt, picked him up, cupped him in a blanket, and held him—skin to skin—on my chest.

That had been our plan all along. Kristin would have a natural birth, and our baby would emerge from the womb and go right onto her breast, where he'd eat for the first time and where he'd hear the heartbeat he'd heard his entire life. That was our plan. Now here I was, with this newborn and no plan. I didn't have a breast, but I had a heart. So I held Ro to it, letting his warmth mix with mine, and I felt him go limp, utterly limp, his entire body softening in a massive sigh. And I held him. He had, after all, done the biggest thing in his entire life. He'd started it.

Fox Lake

When Ro was still a baby, I'd strap him against my chest in one of those wearable carriers and take him on long walks. We'd be belly to belly, his head next to my heart, his legs and arms dangling down. Sometimes he'd nap. Other times he'd just bob along, looking sideways at the thistle and ironweed that fills the ditches along our road or at the odd pickup that clatters by. He likes the weeds that flower.

We live in the foothills of Appalachia, near a lake that nobody goes to. It's called Fox Lake, though we've never seen a fox. In fact, from the road we can't even see the lake. It's hidden behind a half-mile of woods and weed-choked fields. Instead, what we see as we walk along the road—what tells us we're nearing the lake—is an old parking lot, cut into the middle of the woods, in what seems like the middle of nowhere.

The asphalt is cracked. Old beer cans are scattered around, and bits of broken glass glint brown and green in the sunlight. We rarely see anyone parked there, but our neighbors have warned us about the lot: It's where teenagers drink and make out; it's where drug dealers meet buyers; it's where hunters take easy shots from the backs of their trucks. The deer run thick in our woods. Every day at our house we hear rifle shots, in season and out.

Ro and I haven't seen anything so sinister. Once we saw an SUV full of kids blasting music, and once we saw a man wearing a neon-orange camo jumpsuit and carrying a three-foot hunting rifle. I waved. He waved back. That was it. If we see anything at all, it's usually a single car or truck parked in the shade, with a window down or a door opened. Somebody sits there, likely on a lunchbreak, enjoying the breeze and birdsong.

Except once. Once, as Ro and I neared the lot, I saw two men arguing. They'd parked their cars next to each other and stood in the narrow space between them. One man, the one facing us, was much bigger. He had a thick beard and, as he spoke, he jabbed his index finger down at the shorter man. I didn't look at them for long, and they didn't look over, but I'm sure they saw us. We were close enough not to miss.

My plan was to walk one of the trails to the lake. Ro was awake, so I thought we'd sneak up on some geese and send them honking and flapping away. That's big fun for a baby. So I skirted the edge of the lot and took the closest trail. Ro and I disappeared into the overgrown brush, and soon all we could hear were the sparrows and warblers. All, that is, until we heard the gunshots, four of them, loud and close.

I stopped. Adrenaline shot through me. I felt that animal panic: *go, go.* I didn't. Instead, I stood there, doubting my own ears. Gunshots? Really? I looked back. I didn't see or hear anything. Then I looked down at Ro. He was staring in the direction of the shots, his eyes wide and quizzical. He'd heard it, and that was all I needed. I cupped my hands around his small body and took off down the trail.

We'd have to go through the woods. I knew that. Every trail back to the road ended at the parking lot, and we couldn't go back there, because if we did, if we went back, then we'd see—what? One man pointing a gun at another? A body crumpled on the asphalt? These all struck me as Hollywood fantasies, the stuff of second-rate noir. And yet, whatever was happening or had happened, I didn't want us near it.

I cut across a small creek and through some underbrush. Thorns pulled at my legs, and I struggled to keep my footing. I knew the general direction home, but it meant going up, then down a steep hill slick with mossy rocks and last year's leaves. I had to calculate each step. I'd wedge my foot against a weedy outcropping or tree trunk, then lunge for the next handhold, another rock or branch I could use to hoist us up.

The going was slow. Foot to hand, hand to foot. Every so often, I'd stop to check on Ro. He was now dangling right below my chin. And he was fine. In fact, he looked pleasantly surprised. He had a new view of the leaves high above us and the dark intercrossing branches. We were also moving in a novel way, now that I'd become this sort of kangaroo-bear, clambering up the hillside on all fours with my cub in my pouch.

The pace also gave me time to second-guess myself. This was stupid. This wasn't real. This was me, making shit up. Surely, I was overreacting. And wasn't I also putting us in real danger? What if I fell? What if I hurt Ro or myself? Who'd find us this far off the trail? I tried to ignore these thoughts, but before long I couldn't tell if I was dragging us through the woods to avoid danger or just creating it.

I won't detail the long trek back—the difficulty of making my way down the hill, mostly by skidding on my butt, or crossing a stagnant creek that was as much old tires and trash as muck and mud—but I will say that, about halfway down the hill, I heard a car or truck race down the road and screech into the parking lot. I froze and listened, but I couldn't hear anything until a few minutes later, when it sped back in the same direction.

What happened? I don't know. I still don't know. When I finally made it home, filthy and scratched-up, I was so exhausted that I didn't even want to tell Kristin about it. How would I explain what I'd done when I was no longer sure why I'd done it? I did, of course, I told her. And we came to the obvious conclusion that I should drive back to the parking lot and check it out. I handed over Ro and headed back out the door.

On the short drive over, I had one last worry. What if one of the men was still there, waiting for us to come out of the woods? What if this really was one of those get-rid-of-the-body-and-the-witnesses scenarios? Wouldn't I be driving right into it? I turned into the parking lot. It was empty. I drove to the spot where the men had been arguing. No shell casings, no bloody stain. The lot looked the same as it always had.

So I went home. And I more or less forgot about it. And life went on. Since then, Ro and I have gone on that walk once or twice a week. Now, years later, I'll sometimes ask if he remembers that time when we trekked through the woods. Do you remember the climb? The creek? The gunshots? Ro talks now, and he obligingly says, "Yeah," but I doubt he does, just like I now doubt we were really in danger.

And yet those gunshots were real. I know that. I think about that each time we go on our walk after the latest school shooting. I think about how easily I've shrugged off the whole experience, as though it never happened—gone back, in fact, to the very place where it happened, where an angry man fired four gunshots less than a hundred feet from my son. *Here we are,* I think, *right where he or I might have been shot.*

What would it take for me to change? To see the danger we were actually in? To act otherwise? Clearly, what happened wasn't enough. What if I knew we'd see those men again, maybe not today, but soon? Would I still go? Columbine, Virginia Tech, Sandy Hook, Parkland, Uvalde. I know we'll see those men again. We all do. Maybe not today, but soon, and yet we don't change.

I think back to the moment when I was standing on the trail, listening, wondering if the shots I'd heard were real: It wasn't quiet. The birds around us never stopped. The swallows, the warblers, the goldfinches in the high weeds, they all kept singing. For them, gunshots have become normal, natural, a sound as easy to dismiss as the passing trucks or a parent on a walk with his baby or angry armed men, arguing with each other toward who knows what end.

You Are Here

When Ro was almost a year old, I wrote a book for him. He was starting to enjoy books, which at his age meant flipping their pages and chewing on them. His books were simple: a picture of an apple with the word *apple,* a picture of a foot with the word *foot.* I'd read, "Foot!" and squeeze his. I'd read, "Nose!" and squish mine.

I wanted a book that said something more than "spoon," a book that showed him where he was and who he was, a book that showed him the wondrous fact that he was. I was a first-time parent and found myself by turns overjoyed and overwhelmed by this little being who had, in every essential way, blown apart my world.

I had one problem. I can't draw.

Then again, it wasn't as though the drawings in the other books were so great. The pictures were as simple as the words. I thought there might be reasons for this simplicity, so I looked into the research about how babies perceive the world. It turns out their eyesight, like their cognition, is developing. They do see, but only in basic shapes and colors. Sharp contrasts—black against white, red against blue—are what they see best.

So I drew my shapes with these facts in mind. And by "drew," I mean I used PowerPoint. At first, I worked only in pictures, but I soon discovered I needed words. Words are what keep parents from going insane on the fifty-seventh read thought the same picture book. Words give a book its rhythm.

After I finished, I read it to Ro. He seemed to like it, though I had no sense of how it registered for him. What did he see? What did he feel? What is it like to experience a book before we can say "book"?

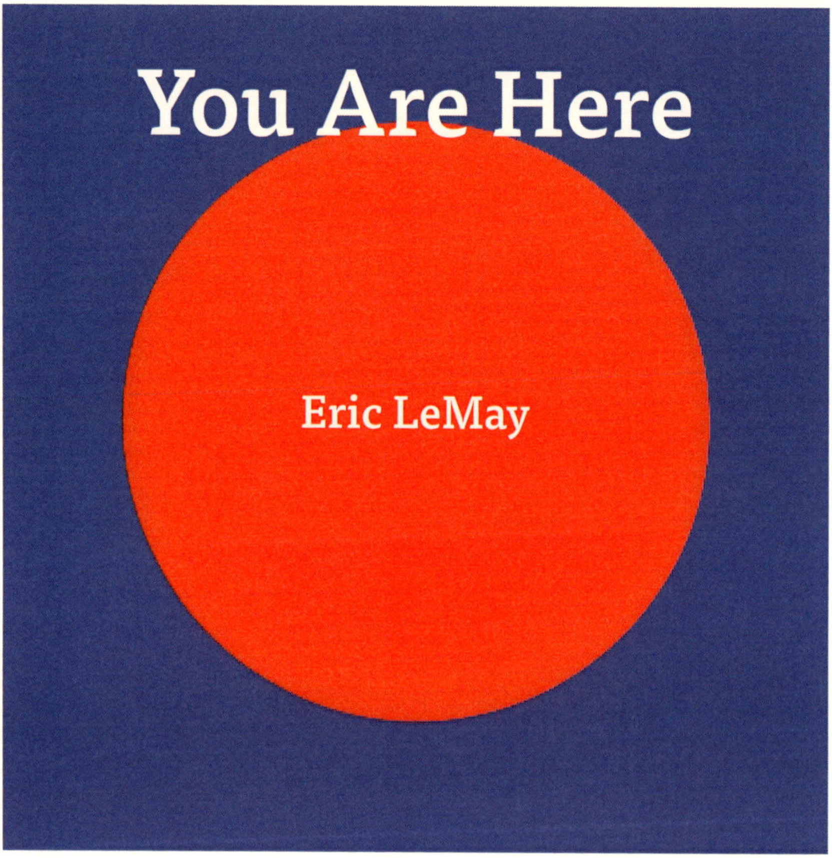
You Are Here
Eric LeMay

First one.

26

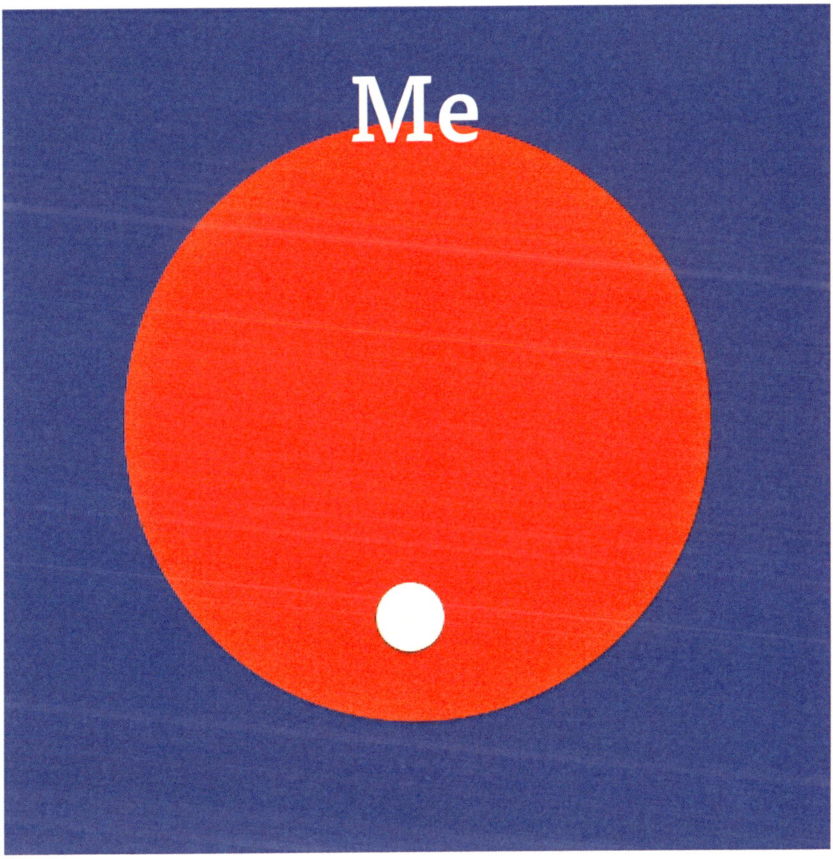
Me

then you.

You

are here.

We are

together

on one

Earth.

Here

we are

near

the sun

among

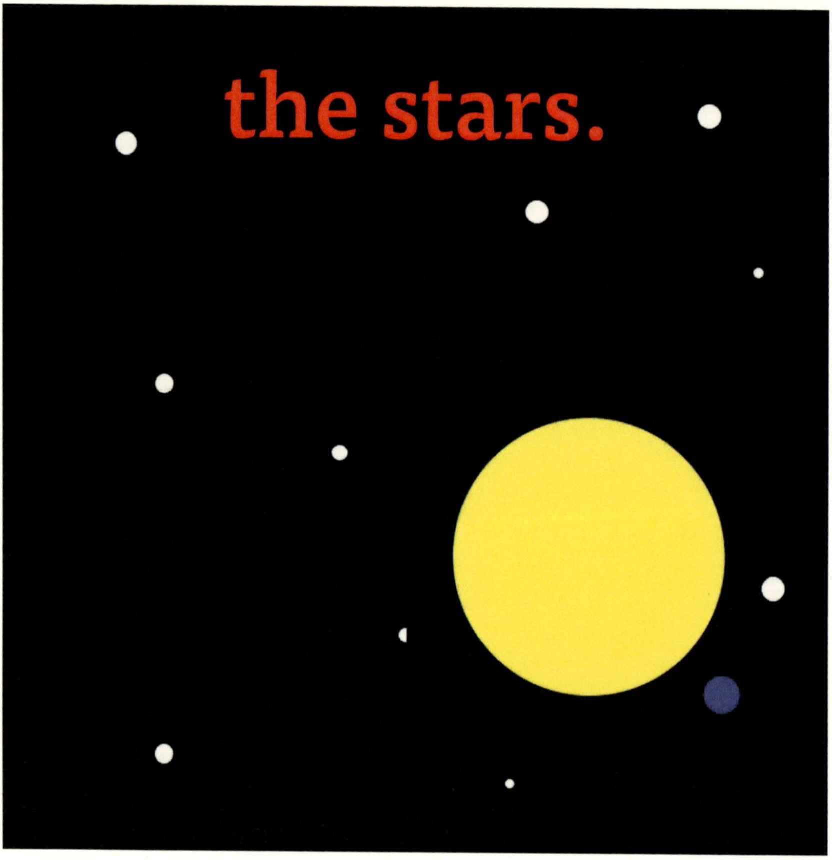
the stars.

41

We are here

Remember Me

Will the memory of me survive my death?

*

Every night, this question stalks me. It prowls the shadows, slit-eyed and restless. It drags its claw across my cheek, settles in my throat, sticks.

I can't answer it. I can't not.

*

Every night, because every night I sleep in a bed with Kristin and Ro. He's there, beside us, between us, on top of us, his arms and legs splayed like a lanky starfish. He's been there since he was born, which is roughly a year before I felt the fleshy mass in the back of my throat.

When it first appeared, I'd lie in bed, swallowing against it, fearing what it was. Now I lie there, knowing, and knowing how every night can become a few nights, too few nights, a last night.

*

After my surgeries—a radical tonsillectomy and selective neck dissection, followed by a second radical tonsillectomy and a second selective neck dissection—I started the monitoring process. I make regular visits to my surgeon. I get MRI and CT scans. I undergo biopsies. I live in a state of constant negation. It's not that I'm cured of cancer. It's that my cancer has not come back.

*

4-15-17

Yesterday, after getting our taxes done, K and I take Ro to Richland Park. He goes down the low curvy slide all by himself, then runs around to do it "again!" He goes down the double slide with K. We watch traffic in the roundabout for "bi-" trucks. A big fuel tanker goes by and honks in response to our waving. Ro: "No!"

Emergency room on Sunday night because my throat is bleeding. Quickly through initial exam, then CT scan, but then wait two hours to find out "tonsillar mass" could be something benign or could be cancer. Home at 3:00 am.

Ro and I at the creek. He throws in big rocks for the splash, climbs up and down the bank, puts leaves in the stream. When they float away, he says, "Bye."

midnight
will be
home.

Michel de Montaigne thought he'd found a way to reckon with death: He created a genre—the essay—that he introduces to his readers as a means of remembering him after he's dead.

In 1580, when he publishes his first book of *Essais,* he introduces it by explaining they're written for his family and friends. The essays, he says, are meant to help them remember him better after he dies. (His death, he adds, "will be soon.") He believes his essays will serve as reminders, refreshers. By reading them, his friends and family will "recover" their knowledge of him, knowledge that would otherwise die along with him.

Through his essays, Montaigne will survive in their memories.

*

It's a thin hope, that an essay can keep you alive in the minds of your readers.

*

It's what I have.

4-23-17

Wednesday morning was my surgical biopsy: pre-op, anesthesia, scope and surgery, post-op. Ro was very stimulated by the clinic. Nurses gave him a surgeon's hat to wear. We played with stickers while waiting. The doctor can't speak to me off his official script. Ro and K both there when I wake.

Ro figured out how to push himself on his trike for first time.

He enjoys saying "ceiling" and "floor." Looks up, looks down. When he says, "heart," K points to hers. "This is the place where mama loves you."

pils are equal, round, and reactive to light.
rmal range of motion.
No thyroid mass
, regular rhythm
heart sounds.
ses are 2+
ses are
ort norm
breath sounds
accessory muscle
has no
has no wheezes.
10:14 AM

Last year, at my grandmother's funeral, I shared her first memory.

She was ninety-eight when she died. No one who came to funeral was near her age. "I'm the only one left," she'd often say. Sometimes sadly, like when she attended her annual high school reunion. Sometimes mater-of-fact, like when I'd ask her about her early life. She'd tell me, for example, about the time she had to throw boiling water on a bull to get it off her front porch or the time, during World War II, when the sheriff came to her door, asking if she'd hidden black-market tires in her house, and how she said, "No, Sheriff, and you come on in and look for yourself," and how the sheriff said, "No, Mary, I trust you," and how he left, and she went in, and right there, where my grandfather had put them without telling her, were the tires, stacked neatly under the piano.

I wonder how many people died in memory when my grandmother died? For how many people was she the last one who remembered them, the only one left?

*

Imagine a timeline. It charts the likelihood that Ro will form a lasting memory of our life together.

Before three, he can't create what psychologists call "episodic memories," those memories that involve specific times and places, people and experiences. He won't, for example, remember me tucking him into the baby carrier and walking him along the snowy trails near our house. He won't remember the fluffy ball I wiggle against his tummy while I sing, "Jelly belly, jelly belly, jelly belly!" or the way he cackles at it. He won't remember the tubes he tried to pull out of the surgical scars in my throat. All of these memories he'll lose, if not immediately, then by the time he's an adolescent.

Not until he's six or seven will he create memories that last. Not until then will the people in his life be those he remembers as the people in his life.

*

Now imagine another timeline. It charts the likelihood that cancer will reappear in my mouth or throat.

During the first year, the chances are highest. If I survive it, my odds improve. Better and better, until the fifth year, when the odds of the cancer returning become statistically negligible.

Ro was one-and-a-half when I underwent treatment for tonsil cancer. He'll be six-and-a-half when I hit that mark, if I hit that mark.

4-30-17

Ro's ability to repeat words is improving. In the right mood, he'll try any words we single out, like when he overheard K say, "Hell no," and said, "Heh nah."

Ro is also learning pronouns. If I say, "Do you want to eat the tomato, or do you want me to eat it?" he'll say, "Me to eat it!" meaning he wants me, his papa, to eat it. Ro always remains "you." (If he'd wanted the tomato, he'd have said, "You to eat it.") Ro hasn't figured out that pronouns switch back and forth.

On Monday, I found out through one of those automatic emails that the tumor is cancer. I spent hours reading up on it and trying to reassure K. Don't see the new surgeon at the James Center until a week from Tuesday, so I have to be patient in all senses.

Summer is here. Eighty-nine degrees today. Hillsides filled with leaves.

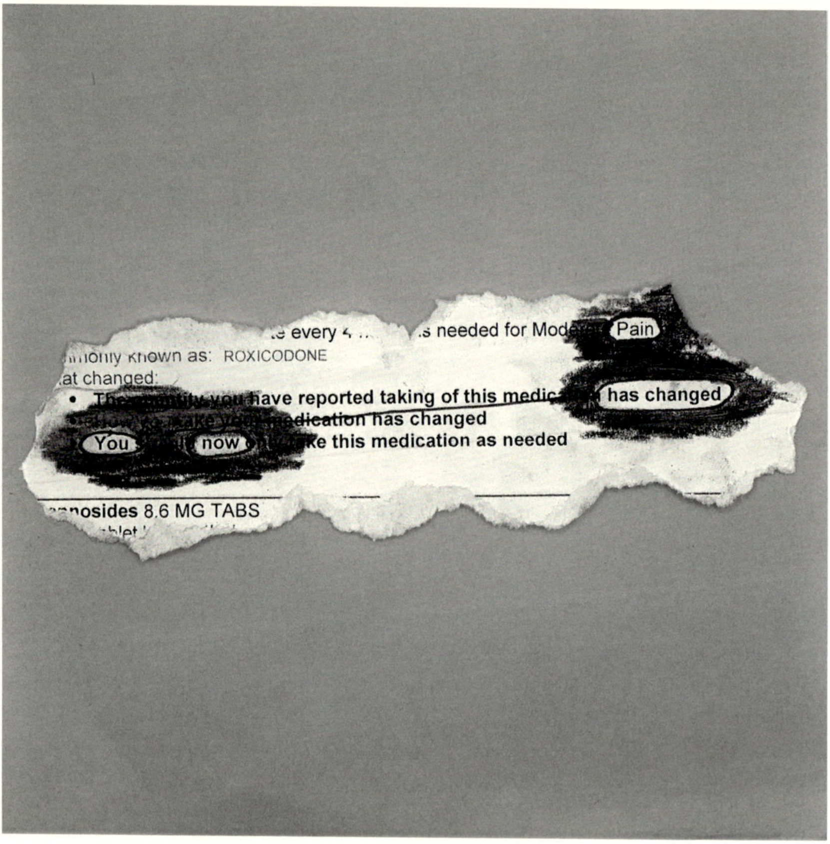
every 4
needed for Mode
Pain
nonly known as: ROXICODONE
at changed:
have reported taking of this medica
has changed
has changed
You
now
this medication as needed
nosides 8.6 MG TABS

"You probably won't find this very comforting," says my surgeon, "but I had a woman come in eight years after her first tumor, and, wouldn't you know it, she had one in the other tonsil. She opted not to do surgery again," he says, waving away what he clearly saw as a bad decision. "She couldn't bear the thought of it."

*

I find what my surgeon says very comforting.

Not because he likes telling me about statistical outliers—the false positives and false negatives that, as a researcher, he finds "interesting"—but because he's the only one who talks to me as if my life is in danger, the only one who recognizes what I must: that my cancer is an open question.

Will it act in a way that's statistically likely, or will it be more interesting?

*

Then again, I might die of some wholly unrelated cause. Or I might not die, at least not now.

I hear my father's voice, saying, as he said while I was waiting for the results of my biopsy, "Might as well put it out of your mind." His advice was well-meant. Why worry about what you can't control? Why suffer through the what-ifs if you don't know what's going to happen? Might as well put it out of your mind.

*

Put it out, like a light, like a candle, like a cat, like a light, put it out, like a light.

*

There's another statistical exception to these timelines. Researchers have found that children as young as two-and-a-half can remember an event if it significantly alters their lives. The examples they give are prolonged hospitalizations or a death in the family.

There's a chance that, if I die, Ro will remember my dying or my death.

*

My grandmother lived to meet Ro. When Kristin and I told her about the baby, she leapt from her couch and shouted, "Now I know why God's been keeping me alive!"

5-7-17

Ro's walk is as much upward as forward. When he runs toward K, each step is a spring. His hair flips up, and he smiles, and he pop-pop-pops ahead. He also hasn't figured out how to move his arms correctly, so they fling out as he steps. His legs are somewhere between a walk and a kick. When I lift him down from something like the swing, he cycles his feet in the air like he's pedaling a bicycle with a tiny front wheel.

I've been researching treatments I may have to undergo. Not pretty. May need a feeding tube inserted into my stomach. May lose my ability to taste, to spit.

Ro goes around the house holding as many ping-pong balls as possible.

ad planned out an
prepped and draped the
down to ysma. Subplatysmal flaps were raised infer
The overlying the sternocleidomastoid mu
nerve was identified in its
cleidomastoid muscle superiorly to the belly
off of the
jugular

Of course, you'd need to know Montaigne. His essays aren't going to help you remember him if you didn't already know him.

*

And if you didn't?

Then Montaigne doesn't see why you'd want to read them. He ends his introduction by saying, "Reader, I myself am the subject of my book: There's no reason you should spend your time on a subject that's so frivolous and vain. So farewell."

That's it. So long, reader. Close Montaigne's book. It's not for you.

*

Montaigne is posturing.

He knows his readers are going to read his essays, whether they know him or not. They have his book, after all. The very fact that he's published it means he's aware he's writing for readers who will never know him.

His posture is a common one for his time, especially if, like him, the author was an aristocrat. Sixteenth-century readers would have expected such authors to make some sort of caveat or disavowal: *I'd never publish this merely for myself, dear reader. I'd never be so vain, so vulgar. I was persuaded to do so—by my friends, by my patron, by my coming death—and even though it's in your hands, it's not worth your time. Farewell.*

No author in Montaigne's time would say: *I desperately need to speak to you, dear reader, so you can hear the voice that's been cut from my throat.*

5-14-17

Ro has discovered "no" not only as a negative assertion but also as a syllable of pleasure. He says "no" to just about everything. Certainly "no" to changing his diaper, but also "no" to factual statements, like "It's raining outside." (Ro: "No.")

On Wednesday, I went up to the James Center for an appointment with my surgeon. A lot of scoping down my nostrils into my throat. A lot of gagging. My research paid off, and I can do surgery without radio or chemo for now. K and I starting to think about how to manage my time in hospital. My parents are going to help and rescheduled their fiftieth anniversary trip to be there. D and N going too. It will be hard. Also haunted by the fact that I am, until the surgery, terminally diseased.

Ro saw a deer last night: "No!"

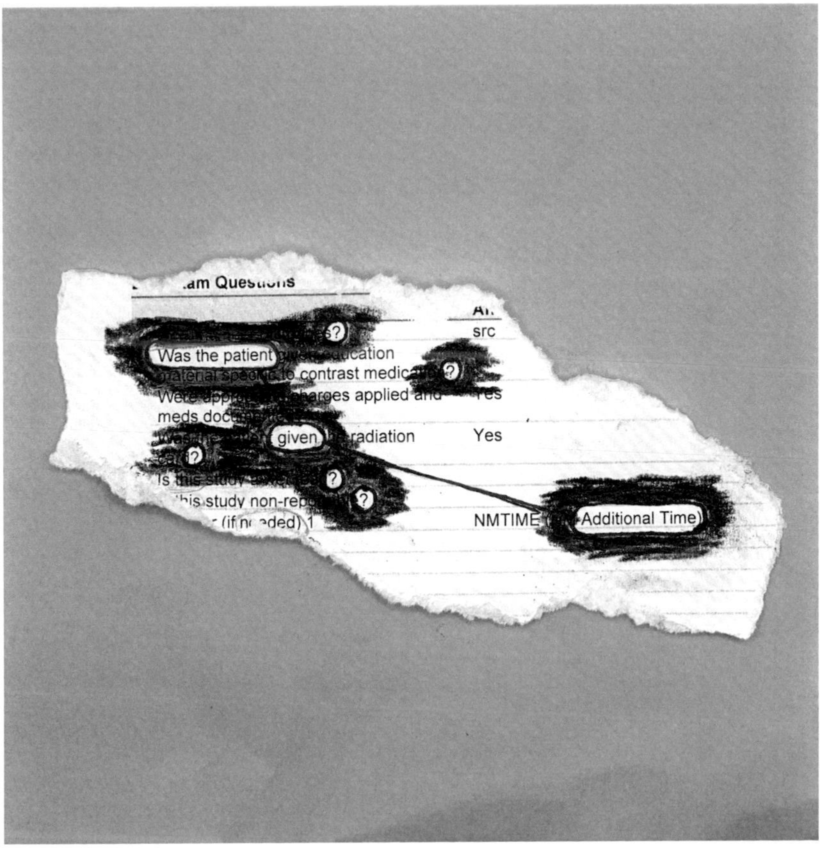
Was the patient
given
Additional Time
?
?
?
?
?
?

We hesitated, Kristin and I, to have Ro sleep with us.

When we first brought him home from the hospital, he was so small, just bones and squeals. We worried we might roll on him, hurt him, or worse. For his own safety, we thought we'd keep him in the crib next to our bed.

*

The decision troubled me.

I'd been reading about what Americans call *co-sleeping.* (The rest of the world doesn't have a term for co-sleeping because, for most of the world, having newborns sleep with their parents is simply the custom. It's simply *sleeping.*) It felt so unnatural to place our son alone in an empty crib after he fell asleep. Eventually, he'd cry. Then Kristin would get up, take him from the crib, nurse him, and put him back in the crib. She'd repeat this pattern throughout the night, through his naps. I'd help as I could. And I'd watch him there, between cries, sleeping on the bare mattress.

*

As I watched, I found myself imagining foxes, apes, lions. Animals, because we're animals.

If I saw a mother ape keep picking up her sleeping baby and putting it somewhere away from her, I'd think there was probably something wrong with the baby. I'd think she was rejecting it. This one doesn't smell right. This one's sick. This is one she's leaving to die.

5-22-17

Ro is now solidly into two-syllable words. He can say in some way almost anything he hears. K put an empty bucket on her head and said, "How do you like my chapeau?" Ro repeated "chapeau" numerous times, as he—and as he instructed us to do—tried on the bucket. Yesterday, when the mail truck arrived, he said, "mailman," though neither K nor I can remember using that word with him. This morning he started using "Roro" to refer to himself with a clarity and consistency we've never seen (all while deciding who should wear the bucket-chapeau).

Ro is consuming large amounts of guacamole and usually has dull green patches on his face where it's dried.

Sometimes surprising things upset him. This morning, when K and I were pushing him on the swing, I suddenly had to jump out of the way so I wouldn't get hit. The urgency on my face caused him to cry.

Negative for bla ce, dysuria
al: Negat pain.
Negati loss of sciousness
Neg memory loss
unology
me: Neg bruises/bleeds easily

During this time, Kristin and I were also being pressured to leave Ro in the crib, even after he woke up, until he cried himself back to sleep.

Most Americans know this treatment as *cry it out.* So long as you know your baby is fed and dry and safe in the crib, you let your baby cry until the crying stops. Eventually, every baby stops crying. Even better, the baby eventually stops crying altogether. That is, after a few nights or weeks of crying it out, your baby learns that you're not going to come and stops crying out for you.

After that, the baby spends every night quietly sleeping, or if not sleeping, then quiet, and you get to sleep.

*

The parents who'd done this to their babies gave us all sorts of advice. We could shut the door. We could wear headphones. We could put Ro's crib in another part of the house, far away from our bedroom, where we wouldn't hear him cry.

The mothers who urged us to "cry it out" all agreed: Hearing your baby scream was horrible. The fathers had an easier time. My father-in-law, for example, told us just to ignore it. Another father told us how on the first night his son never fell asleep. He kept crying all night long. "That must have been hard," I said. "Yeah," he sighed, "I felt sorry for the neighbors."

*

It's not clear what the *it* in *cry it out* refers to.

*

It, the night. *It,* your tears. *It,* your trust, your terror, your hope that if you ever need someone when you cry out in the night, someone will come.

5-28-17

Ro is now very interested in his first baby book. We look through it, picture by picture. This happens at a time when he's also interested in other babies. The other day at the gym, he climbed into another child's carrier, and we played "Baby Roland," where he "slept" by stiffening his arms and legs and staying very, very still as I rocked him. After we played this once, he wanted to play it the entire time.

We went for a family walk—Ro loves being in the "bak pa!" Grass and weeds hip-high. K pulled honeysuckle blossoms. All of us tasted the sweet nectar inside.

y and sent off fo
ack of a
suture.
then
for the der
ted the
without any
atient
gently
rom an
on. Dr.
present
47 PM
17 10:58 AM

My grandmother was born in 1918.

When I asked her about her very first memory—the first thing she could ever remember happening—she recalled it immediately. Her face brightened, and she started telling me about it. When she finished, I asked her how old she was at the time. She paused for a second. "I'd say three or four." That meant 1921 or 1922.

I felt so lucky to be there, to hear this memory from almost a hundred years ago, to glimpse this self from my grandmother's past, arriving to say hello again, to say, however briefly, "I'm you again."

*

How many times will you relive your most distant memories, your most distant selves? How many times will you revisit being three or four? How many times is enough?

*

When my grandmother was a girl, she lived on a farm. Along the back field of that farm ran the railroad. One day, a train stopped there. She went out to meet it with her father and her older brother and saw some of the crew exiting the train. A few of them started talking with her father, and at some point, two porters asked her if she'd like to see the train. She must have said yes, because the porters lifted her and her brother onto their shoulders and carried them onto the train.

The porters took them through the dining car, through the kitchen car, and into the pantry car. One of the porters told my grandmother, "Open that bin there." She did, but she didn't know what was inside. "Now take a big handful," said the porter. She did. She stretched her arm as far as she could into the bin, closed her fingers, and pulled out a huge handful of dried coconut.

How sweet it must have been. How unlikely.

6-4-17

Ro is becoming more involved and directive in his eating, wanting to "ho" the spoon or fork, asking for water or a new cup or juice by signing. He's also throwing food and spitting water. The basic arc is that at the beginning of the meal he's hungry and focuses on eating, but as he gets full the food and eating experience becomes more about other activities: play, testing, using his pincer grip. He's getting better at picking up and maneuvering bites. Blackberries, for example. This week, he's shown an appetite for watermelon chunks.

Went to the James Center on Tuesday for pre-op and PET scan. No clear evidence the cancer has spread. Trying to get prepped in the next three days for surgery.

Within this
gross
appear normal.
appear normal.
appearance.

Montaigne is posturing, but he's also right: Whether or not you know the essayist changes your experience of reading an essay.

If, for example, you read Montaigne now, you don't encounter a person, but a persona. You meet a Montaigne, to be sure, but this Montaigne is a literary trick, a pseudo-self, brought to life as much by you as by him. Your intelligence, your psychology, your expectations animate his essays, which are, after all, just words. The only living person around for this encounter is you. You might be reading the same essays that other readers have read, but the persona you're experiencing—the Montaigne who appears to you in and across the essays—is uniquely yours and, in many ways, uniquely you.

Recall that *persona* comes from the Latin for *mask,* like those worn by actors in classical Greek dramas. When you pull back Montaigne's mask, you don't find Montaigne. You find you.

*

Yet, if you knew Montaigne, the flesh-and-blood man who lived and died on his estate near Bordeaux, you'd find the person in the persona. You'd bring your knowledge of him to his essays. Is this the man I know? And if not, then how do I reconcile the man I know with the words I read? Which is true? Which is truer?

If you knew Montaigne, person and personae would meet, merge, even clash, and you'd finish the essay with a different, perhaps a deeper understanding of Montaigne, who might now strike you less like a person than a persona hidden behind a person. That is, having known Montaigne and having read Montaigne, you might find that the true man lies not so much in his flesh-and-blood presence as in his essays.

When you know the essayist, the essay often seems to reveal a deeper truth, a truer self.

6-14-17

Arrived at the James Center and very quickly went up to surgery. K stayed with me and cracked jokes as nurses, anesthesiologists, and surgeons cycled through. Said goodbye to K, who took Ro to the hotel for nap.

Wheeled into operating room. The surgical robot was much larger than I expected, more like a machine for moving cargo. Various computer monitors. Clamps and instruments. A nurse held my hand. Whiteboard with timelines of procedures. I don't remember dropping off.

Came to with post-op staff. Sensation of removing catheter was first. Not a very nice nurse. No one spoke to me. Heard commotion of other patients coming in and out. Eventually wheeled to my room by someone who wasn't supposed to do it, a janitor. Room on twenty-first floor. K and parents come in to say hello. K says I don't look that bad so brings back Ro to see me. We sing "Twinkle, Twinkle, Little Star."

Then starts longest night. Hooked up to two IVs, one for fluids, one for antibiotic. Also drainage tube in neck. Very hard to move. I mistakenly thought I was on a painkiller drip, so stuck with ice chips. Only at some point in middle of the night did the nurse tell me painkillers are by request only. "Do you want a Tylenol?" Yes. Later nurse threatens to put back in catheter if I don't pee enough. I spend hours standing in the dark on shaky legs, squeezing out drops until my stomach cramps. Not enough. Then force myself into hourly cycle of painfully gulping water and trying to pee, each time having to roll off covers, manage three tubes, stand in freezing dark, shaking, trying to pee into a plastic container.

At 6:00 am interns come in and report on surgery: No noticeable tumors found in neck and surgeon removed both tonsils. I ask why? No compelling reason except surgeon was "already there." Good news of possibly going home in a day.

Family visits. Ro obviously tired. Yesterday was his longest day, literally. He didn't fall asleep until 11:00 pm. By all reports, he did very well. He walked loops around the waiting room, saying "Hi" to everyone.

ATTENDING
I was
sent and personally performed the key and critical
with
portions of an
was also immediately
my absence.

The official term for *cry it out,* the one used by researchers and sleep trainers, is *extinction.*

I learned it from one of the articles my father-in-law kept emailing us. He's wanted us to leave Ro crying from the moment he was born. When he visited us in the hospital, he turned to me, father to father, and said, "Sometimes you just let them cry."

*

Since I've had cancer, I cry.

I try not to, but the tears come. I tilt my eyes, as though I can reabsorb them. I press my fingers to my tear ducts. I sniff, haphazardly. When I'm not crying, I feel like I am. I feel like I'm living in that moment right before you cry, when you know you might be able to stop, but can't. I feel like I'm made of tears, tears masquerading as a self.

*

We aren't going to leave our son alone, Kristin and I, crying for us in the dark. We're going keep him close, animals we are, animals we are.

6-18-17

Yesterday was Ro's first time on his wagon. He liked it very much, especially the moment when the pulling starts. I pulled him around the yard and up and down the driveway. Then we put rocks inside it. Rocks, for Ro, can go in anything: buckets, trucks, hands. Our porch and yard are now hard to walk on because of all the rocks he's moved there from the driveway.

Emotionally and physically wrecked and trying to recover.

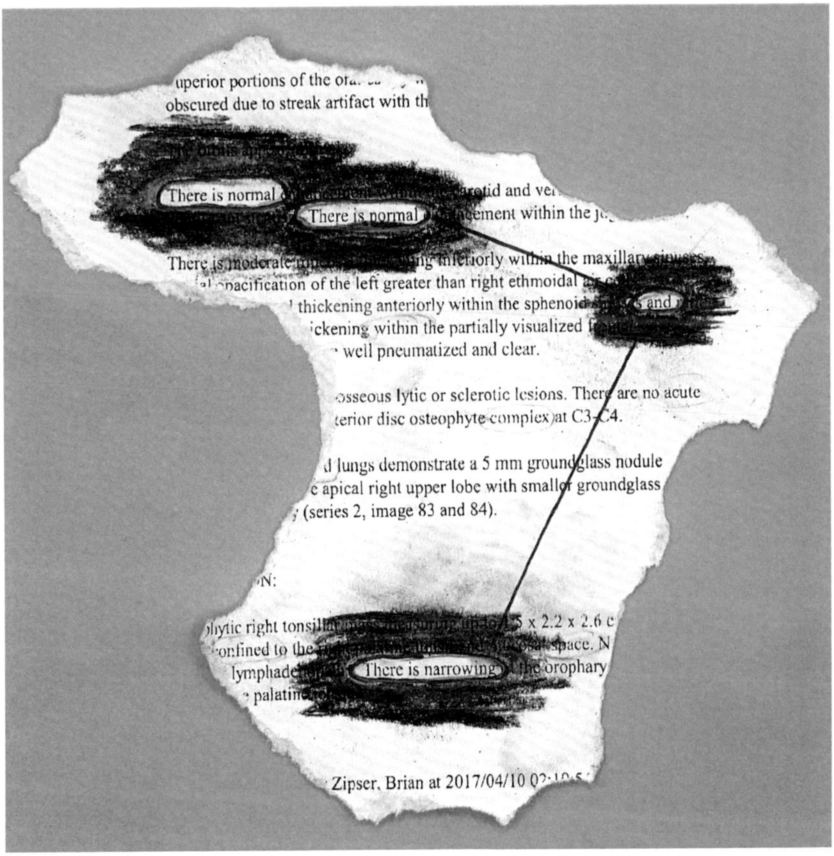
uperior portions of the ora
obscured due to streak artifact with th
There is normal
arotid and ve
There is normal
ement within the j
There is moderate
inferiorly within the maxillary sinuses
pacification of the left greater than right ethmoidal
thickening anteriorly within the sphenoid
and
ckening within the partially visualized
well pneumatized and clear.
osseous lytic or sclerotic lesions. There are no acute
terior disc osteophyte complex at C3-C4.
d lungs demonstrate a 5 mm groundglass nodule
c apical right upper lobe with smaller groundglass
(series 2, image 83 and 84).
N:
hytic right tonsil
5 x 2.2 x 2.6 c
onfined to the
space. N
lymphade
There is narrowing
the orophary
palatine
Zipser, Brian at 2017/04/10

When Ro was almost two, we started playing a game we call "Recitation."

I hold him in front of the bathroom mirror, then we make grand theatrical gestures and quote from Shakespeare. "To be!" I say. "To be!" he says. "Or not to be," I say. "Or not to be!" he says. On we go, until we're done. Then we flourish our hands, and he usually shouts, "Again!"

We do *Richard III* and lines from the *Sonnets,* but we always come back to *Hamlet.* It's the play I know best. I've read it for decades and, as a writer, created variations of it. I'm not alone. From Melville to Eliot to Stoppard, there's a long line of writers, mostly white men, who've riffed on the play, usually to see what they could find of themselves in Shakespeare's most thought-laden character. That's how I'd always approached it: I saw myself as Hamlet.

Now, when I hold my son in my arms and we do our little version of the play, I realize he's Hamlet. I'm the father in the play, the dead father. I'm the ghost.

6-25-17

Ro is becoming bold. He stands and pivots on the slide, uses only his arms to support himself, and dangles his feet. He climbs the big ladder at the playground, goes charging toward the stairs on the porch. He thinks he's fully in control, but he's not there yet, so lots of falls and bonks. He's been climbing, for example, on the couches for weeks and hasn't had any trouble, but he's fallen off all of them this week, including a nearly 360° fall where he landed on his back. K and I were more scared than Ro.

On Tuesday I got the pathology reports. I had a second tumor in the other tonsil, the one removed because the surgeon was there. I will need to go through all the same surgeries again—mouth, neck—on the opposite side. I went back up to the James Center on Wednesday. My surgeon has a flare for the dramatic. "Will we be able to get away without radiating you?" Long pause. "I don't know."

Height of summer. Solstice.

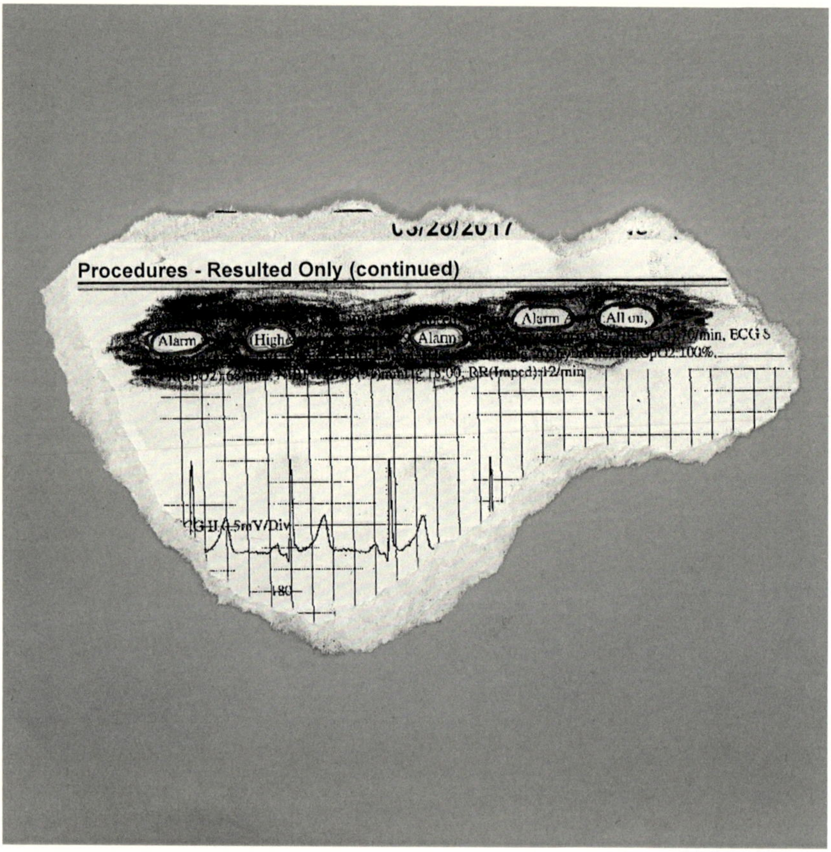
Procedures - Resulted Only (continued)
Alarm
High
Alarm
Alarm
All on,

I haven't been able to write since I was diagnosed.

What do you write about—what thoughts do you express, what memories do you set down—when everything is weighted with last?

*

Instead, I've kept a journal.

About once a week, I write down our highlights: story time at the library, meltdowns at gymnastics. I note developments: new words, new wonders, worries, joys. Sometimes I focus on a specific thing. This is how we go to bed. This is how we choose our socks. Other times I make lists. These are the mushrooms we stomp in the pine grove. These are the stuffed animals we like right now.

I'm hoping these small entries amount to a larger picture of our lives, that from these everyday events, Ro might see us for who we are, who we were.

*

A final thing about Montaigne: The essay, as he created it, doesn't need closure.

In his essays, Montaigne makes discoveries, he surprises himself, but he doesn't feel the need for his writing to amount to anything more than trials, attempts, tests—those original meanings of the term he chose for them: *essays*. For Montaigne, an essay achieves its aim if he reckons with what he knows or thought he knew or doesn't know or can't.

An essay can end as open, as unsettled, as it began.

7-4-17

Had both surgeries again: a lot of "same as" last time. Everyone rallies and comes again. Surgical room once again same setup. Same pre-op. Don't recall holding area on wakeup. In room, K came back, then parents, then K and Ro. Quick hellos. First night horrible. Threw up multiple times and exhausted from straining to pee. No sleep. In morning, everyone visits. Ro likes using privacy curtain to play hide-and-seek. He also enjoys riding on the IV cart. K reports that Ro once again said "Hi!" to everyone in the waiting room. Four people in a group, four *hi*'s. Feeling the same pain in recovery. Doped up and fatigued.

Right now Ro and K are at the parade.

No results on pathologies.

Ro currently has a big blue streak on the back of his calf from picking brambleberries in the field, wiping the juice on his legs.

the patien
we are recommendi
the patient he is willing to ta
close follow up. Thank you
any questions in the inte please do not
Depart Radiation Oncology
Electronicall

Since Ro was born, I've become acutely aware of how much I am not myself, how much, that is, I am my parents.

*

I'd imagined this would happen. It's a truism: When you become a parent, you become your parents. I expected, in becoming a father, to become mine.

What I hadn't imagined was the scope of it, that my son's birth would trigger in me so many of my father's personality traits, and not only his but also my mother's and grandmothers' and grandfathers' and that these, in turn, must have come from their parents and their parents' parents, on and on, back through generations, all of these personality traits passing from body to body, combining and recombining into self after self, as distinct—if you could track them—as the genes you inherit from those ancestors you'll never know.

Before Ro was born, I hadn't imagined how many selves inhabit me.

*

Yet I myself am the subject of my book.

And through it I'm trying to find the self I hope to be, the self my son may one day become.

*

This isn't the first time I've tried. Since I've gotten sick, I've tried to write and rewrite my life as it is now.

I spent all of last winter rewriting a single essay. I called it "Remember Me." That's what the ghost of Hamlet's father says to Hamlet before he disappears. I'd wake up in the dark and leave Kristin and Ro together in bed. Then I'd sit on the couch, trying to conjure up what was in me.

I kept working on it, in sentences that would rise and convulse and ultimately collapse. I worked across more appointments, more biopsies, more scans, across months of waiting to know if the cancer had come back. I wrote it and rewrote it and finally I quit.

*

What did you try to say?

I tried to say: Here, my heart, myself, my son, I am here.

7-9-17

On Monday, Dad took me up to the James Center to have the drain removed from my neck. A very long drive for him. He made it clear he was glad to do it. Didn't get to see the surgeon. Instead, the nurse says to me, "Breath out on three . . . " and then, on three, I feel her pull the tube out of my throat.

Got results from pathologies the next day. No cancer.

Heavy rainstorms this week. During the thunder, I took Ro onto the porch. (Ro: "No thunder!") Fallen branches. High winds. Lights flicking. Thought we were going to lose power, but held on.

The wound
was turned over
and remained

Remember Me

I have cancer. One tumor, then another, masses at the back of my throat, like words I can't swallow or speak. I have a prognosis. A 56 percent chance, an 80 percent chance, a 93 percent chance of surviving the next five years.

"Depends on the study," says my surgeon. "We'll see," he says.

I have a son. He's almost two. He hasn't learned how pronouns work. "Do you want a snack?" I ask. "You want a clementine," he answers. "Do you want me to peel it?" I ask. "Me to peel it," he answers. I tear off the bright orange skin and give it to him. I have a son who, in syntax, if not in fact, hasn't divided I from you from me.

"You need some love," he says. "You need more clementine."

I have fears. So many fears. I fear, for example, that I will die and that my son will forget me. He's too young to create memories that last. He will have photos, yes, and videos, yes, but I fear he will have no living memory of me. No sight he knows he saw, no touch he knows he felt. I fear I will die in my son's mind.

"Remember me," says the ghost of Hamlet's father.

He's died too soon, and he returns in the night full of desires for this world. He wants more violence, more death. His last words to his son are not so much a command as a plea.

"Hamlet," he says, "remember me."

I have two scars. Slits along my neck. My surgeon opened one side, then another, removing tissue that might hold more cancer. I have no feeling between them, only a tightness, like a choke, like fingers lodged around my throat.

"Those nerves in the neck don't like to be messed with," says my surgeon. "It'll probably improve," he says, "or not."

I have an image of my son. He's eight, he's seventeen, he's forty-three. He's looking in the mirror, and he's trying to subtract the features on his face that are his mother's, features he knows. He's trying to see how much of him is me, is you, is I?

"Remember me," says the ghost, fading with the dawn.

I, too, have desires. I do not want to die. I do not want to haunt my son in this world or the next. Every morning, I hold him close. He wriggles and he fusses. He needs another clementine. I let him go. I watch you go.

"Remember me," I want to say, because I want you to remember me, as I love you now and as I'd love you then, in that unknown future, when it comes and I am not.

OSA: no
Risk Ass
Do you
- No
Are you
ntly tir
Have you
n obse
igh blo
more
n 50? -
? - No
Neck circumference g
Neck Circumference
more then 35?

*

Hole

A year into the pandemic, as the earth grew pocked with graves and March slung its low, gray sky over the woods behind our house, Ro and I went out into the rain and dug a hole. We'd exhausted every game, every book. Why not dig in the cold, wet dirt? I stomped on the shovel, tearing up the dead grass. Rain streaked down his flimsy plastic jacket.

"Will we find treasure?" he asked.

After we'd dug for a while, I took a dime from the change I'd brought and dropped it into the hole. "See if there's treasure," I said. He knelt down and pinched out the rain-slick dime.

He gleamed. "Do you think there's more?"

I turned over a shovelful of dirt, then held out a quarter and dropped it, but this time he watched me, watched as I dropped the quarter into the hole, and it stuck.

"Look," he said, "more treasure."

On we went, me dropping coins, him watching me drop them, then picking them out from the muddy clods. His fingers grew blacker and blacker. Soon he had too many coins to hold. Would I hold them for him? I did, and then I began dropping those same coins back into our hole.

I wanted to keep our game—if it was a game—alive.

Text Our Dead

December 2020 through February 2021

How will we mourn everyone who's dead and dying?

Every day, I look at the new numbers. Yesterday's death count, in my county, our country, our world. As though I'm not numb to them. Morgue fatigue, magnitude fatigue. I move to metaphors: yesterday another 9/11, another Antietam. One jumbo jet going down, two going down, the *Titanic* going down. I try to hold the whole of it in my head and can't. Bodies in mass graves. Bodies in refrigerator trucks.

And all this happening while so many Americans refuse to see it's happening. Since it started, two of my uncles have died. Both with severe comorbidities, both in care facilities, though one returned home to die in hospice. I can't get a clear answer about whether their deaths were COVID-related. Most of my family veers right, sees the virus as a political exaggeration. Even mentioning it is charged.

"What happened?" I ask my father on the phone. "Well, it's not entirely clear. He was in bad shape." I know not to press him, not because my father isn't reasonable, but because he knows better than to press our family about the virus at such a moment. This, in our family etiquette, isn't a moment for politics.

How will we mourn our dead when we can't speak about how they died or how, had we acted otherwise as a country, so many of them wouldn't have?

Sometimes I try to still these questions looping in my head by listening to podcasts, usually in dark, sleepless hours. Experts on collective trauma, storytellers on healing, gurus on grief. Sometimes it helps. One night, I came across a story about Itaru Sasaki.

Sasaki is a garden designer. In 2010, he built one of those old-timey telephone booths in his garden. It overlooks the sea in the Otsuchi region on the east coast of Japan. In the booth is a black rotary phone. The phone isn't connected to anything. No line, no signal. Sasaki built it after his cousin who was also his longtime drinking buddy died of cancer. He uses the phone to speak to his dead cousin. Sasaki calls it *kaze no denwa, the wind phone* or *the phone of the wind.* It's the wind that carries your words to the dead.

And then, about a year later, on March 11, 2011, one of the worst tsunamis in history hit the eastern coast of Japan, the very region where Sasaki lives. At least 16,000 people died, another 2,500 went missing, almost half a million were displaced. Soon after, the wind phone became a place of pilgrimage. Thousands of people have come to Sasaki's garden, picked up the black telephone, and called their dead.

In the podcast, I heard the mourners speaking on the phone. I heard the grief rake through their voices. As I was listening and crying and trying not to wake up Kristin and Ro sleeping next to me, I found myself wondering what a wind phone might look like for me? For us? What might carry our words to our dead?

Then it occurred to me: We don't call, we text. What if we could text our dead? So I did what you do with a grief-soaked idea that comes to you on a sleepless night in the middle of a global pandemic. I registered an internet domain, built a website, bought a phone, got a new line, and created Text Our Dead, where you can send a text to your dead.

Here is how I introduce it:

> Q: What is this?
>
> This is a chance to text someone who has died.
>
> Q: What should I text?

> Text what you want to say. Or what you didn't. Ask what you want to ask. Or didn't. Text about your dreams or your day or your dog. Send a blessing. Send a curse. Share with your dead your grief, your memories, your love.
>
> Q: Will I get a text back?
>
> Not from this number, which isn't the same as saying you won't hear back.

In the daylight, I doubt the idea holds up. Then again, right now I doubt anything holds up, including me.

Sometimes, I think of Text Our Dead as an intervention into the way we mourn as Americans. Even without a pandemic, our mourning rituals are terrible. Be brave at the funeral. Be back at work on Monday. Get over it. Get on with it. Don't cry. Don't bury your loved ones in your heart. We're bad at death, bad with our dead, and bad deaths are happening all around us. We can't even get together and cry right now, much less hold a visitation or a funeral.

Like Sasaki's phone, Text Our Dead offers us a different way to mourn, one that doesn't cut us off from our dead. "Life," says Sasaki, "is only, at most, 100 years. But death is something that goes on much longer, both for the person who has died and also for the survivors, who must find a way to feel connected to the dead. Death does not end the life. All the people who are left afterward are still figuring out what to do about it. They need a way to feel connected." For Sasaki, death goes on, life goes on, and the living need to feel connected to the dead.

How might this happen for us? Maybe through our smartphones rather than Sasaki's old rotary phone. When asked why he chose a phone, Sasaki explained that picking up the phone primes you to speak. You just start talking. That's right as far as it goes, but nowadays we just start texting. It's our go-to, our most likely way of connecting with others in our lives. Maybe texting can also connect us with our dead.

Our phones, after all, are already conduits of death. The final calls from the ICU, the last FaceTimes. At this moment, it's the closest thing many of us have to human touch. Touchscreens. What's left to lose?

Here is the text I sent to one of my uncles:

> I know so little about your life. My mother told me you grew up in the Kentucky hills in a large family where no one had their own bed. You slept where you could. My father told me your father drove a dynamite truck. This is so little, and still it leads me to wonder: Is this why you could never stand still? Is this why your life blew up?

As a writer, I believe in words, even words thumbed on our phones and mangled by autocorrect. From words, we craft our memories, our missing. From words, we summon our dead.

Here is the text I sent to my other uncle:

> I'm thinking about your hands. Massive carpenter's hands. That was our thing: you teaching me how to shake hands, like men should, and me, just a kid, pretending to learn, as though one day I'd have your giant's grip. I was told that when you died, you'd shrunken to half yourself, bedridden for years. I'm an uncle now. Nephews and nieces, and with not one of them do I have a thing, a single thing. I can hear your voice so easily. It is full of sweet wood.

"Death does not end the life," says Sasaki. For us, this sounds absurd. It asks us to change our sense of death in a powerful, perhaps even impossible way. And yet, if we're willing do something as absurd as risk our lives and the lives of others texting in traffic, why not risk the absurdity of texting our dead?

In an interview I did about the project for Wisconsin Public Radio, the host asked me what sort of texts people sent. "A lot of grief," I said. "A lot of missing. *Missing* is probably the word that comes up the most. But also memories. . . . *I remember our 54th wedding anniversary . . . I haven't forgotten you . . .* " I wish I'd also told him how fortunate I felt to read these texts, to overhear these words to those we haven't forgotten.

On the website, I end the introduction to Text Our Dead with a final question:

> Q: Is there anything else I should ask?
>
> When you die—and you will—what will you hope to hear from the living?

1-13-21

US Daily Deaths

1-1-21: 2,557

1-2-21: 2,406

1-3-21: 1,435

1-4-21: 1,547

1-5-21: 3,484

1-6-21: 3,902

1-7-21: 4,079

1-8-21: 3,780

1-9-21: 3,523

1-10-21: 2,058

1-11-21: 1,733

1-12-21: 4,064

1-13-21: 4,022

1-14-21: 3,915

1-15-21: 3,679

"Daddy's in the hospital."

Over the phone, my mother's voice is a cracked and hollow bone. Outside, the moon is buried in clouds.

I have never in my life called my father "Daddy." This is what my mother does when she can't handle what's happening. She speaks as though I'm a child in a children's story, the one she's telling herself ends happily. This is the winter of the pandemic, and 400,000 dead Americans. Stories that begin in the emergency room aren't ending happily.

As she speaks, I listen for facts about my father's condition, and they tangle in my head with what I already know. My father is eighty-one. My father has a heart condition. My father and my mother go out every day, sometimes with masks, sometimes not.

"He walked in and he said, 'Jerri, I think I need to go to the hospital.' He said he's never felt like this. He was gray, absolutely gray. He said

On the night she calls, I am preparing to leave the next morning for my regular cancer screening at the James Center, where I've been cut open six times for the same cancer, first when my son was just over a year old.

I sleep fitfully and leave in the winter dark. I drive north, angry at my father. Worried for him.

When I arrive, I call my mother from the parking garage.

1-16-21: 3,709

1-17-21: 2,053

1-18-21: 1,395

1-19-21: 2,141

1-20-21: 4,409

1-21-21: 3,878

1-22-21: 3,980

1-23-21: 3,577

1-24-21: 1,940

1-25-21: 1,539

1-26-21: 3,734

1-27-21: 4,077

1-28-21: 4,011

1-29-21: 3,503

1-30-21: 2,982

1-31-21: 2,059

his chest was constricted and he couldn't breathe. The nurse wasn't very nice. It might have been the end of her shift. She said I couldn't stay because of the—because of—everything."

The *everything* is the pandemic and everything it's done to us, all of us. My mother can't name it, because she believes that if she does, then this is it. My father will have the virus and he'll die.

And that's what I'm thinking. This is it. This is another of the thousands of deaths that are happening every day, and this death will be my father's.

"He said to me, 'Don't tell Eric and Dave,' but I thought I should."

Eric and Dave. That's me. That's my brother. He said not to tell us. Now I'm the one who can't handle what's happening. If it were up to my father, my brother and I would be having another typical night in our endless nights of lockdown, and my father and mother would be going through all of this alone, he in an ER bed and she in their suddenly all-too-quiet house. If it were up to my father, the call I'd eventually get from my mother might start, "Daddy's dead."

As we talk, I realize I haven't told her or my father about this screening or any screenings in which I do or don't find out I have cancer.

I've told myself I don't want to worry them, there's no reason to worry them, not until there's a reason to worry.

We are a family of silences, unto death.

We are a family that doesn't love one another enough. Or too much.

In that same garage, the sun lighting up the exhaust-blown city, I remem-

It will take less than twenty-four hours for me to feel the absurd thankfulness that my father has only gone through a cardiac episode. My father does not have COVID-19. My father will live. He gets tested and retested and goes home the very next day.

And it's in those same twenty-four hours that it strikes me: All this has been a dry run for his death to come, whether it's from the virus or not, whether it's in the emergency room or not. Nothing is going to change about who my father is, about who my mother is. My father will not want me to know when he is dying until after he's dead, and my mother will tell a story over his dying and his death, one that somehow ends happily.

And those of us who are left will live in the ever after of it all.

ber holding my son before my first surgery, holding him and, with him, the possibility of my own death.

I, too, would have sought to die away from him. I, too, would have called that, as I'm sure my father would, *sparing him.*

No last look, no last touch, no chance to whisper into his small bones in a way his bones might remember, "I love you."

How spare, how terribly spare that death would be.

Sorrow-Borne

Butcher paper, peanut butter, birdseed, 4' x 16' pine boards

A series of poems created out of birdseed and performed by chickadees, titmice, woodpeckers, cardinals, bluejays, and other nonhuman collaborators. The birds dismantle and consume the poems and, in so doing, transform their energy and meaning from human to avian, from text to flight, flesh, and shit, which in turn enriches the soil out of which grow the peanuts, cracked corn, wheat, milo, safflower, black-oil sunflower, and other seeds from which the poems are made.

WEEP TO OPEN IN
A DARKER   EARTH
WEEP   TO THE WIND TO
SWALLOW OUR   NAMES

(When I wrote these poems, I imagined how the birds would dismantle them, seed by seed. I likened them to Tibetan prayer flags: the way the wind carries off the prayers inscribed on them until, finally, the flags are in tatters and the prayers are pure spirit. I made these poems, these prayers, for me, for the birds, for this earth we are.)

WE LIVED SO LONG IN
SIDE US LIKE ICE
ON BLACK SEAS
ALIVE AND NOT TO LAST

(To begin each poem, I'd unroll a huge sheet of butcher paper across the floor and stencil the words onto it. I'd use large block letters. As I worked, I'd end up memorizing the poem, repeating each word as I penciled it into being. It felt mediative, but also achy. I'd kneel on the floor for hours. I ended up buying kneepads from the hardware store.)

LET LUSH OVERCOME US
LET LIGHT STAIN US
A STAR
CASTS OUR SHADOW

(The next morning, I'd go into the woods with two giant boards and four sawhorses. The boards were hard to carry through the trees. The sawhorses were old and wobbly. I'd set everything up, then cover the boards with the butcher paper. On windy days, it would billow like a giant sail that I'd fight to tape down.)

NOW THE BODIES
IN THE WINTER GROUND
NOW BONE SONGS
OUR ONLY SONGS

(Then I'd fill in the outlines of the letters with peanut butter. I'd use my fingers, smearing it along the curves of the words, occasionally taking a lick. Once I'd done every letter, I'd circle back, my fingers numb from the cold, and sprinkle them with birdseed, pressing it in so it'd stick. I'd finish around sunset, surrounded by birds.)

THIS SUN BURNING IN
THIS SKY WE CRY
OUT WE ALSO BURN
ALSO RISE

(As the sky pinkened, I'd step back and watch the birds pick apart the poem. They'd been there all along, of course, watching from the trees. If I took a break, they'd sweep in and start eating letters. For them, I was creating not a poem but a feast. I'd set a massive table in the middle of the woods in the middle of winter. They wanted me to leave it to them.)

BY DAZZLE WE ARE MEANT
TO SEE MEANT
TO BE
MORE THAN OUR MARROW

(And I did. I'd leave the poem for a few days. Sometimes it would rain or snow. The seeds would slowly disappear. The birds would visit less and less. The poem would fade into faint outlines of peanut oil, or the wind would rip it, or a possum would gnaw it into a mess. Later, I'd burn the leftover paper. I'd watch it waft away as smoke.)

NEARER THAN EVER
LASTING DEATH
BECKONS US
TO TAKE WING YES

(One day, I wrote an artist's description, the one at the start of these poems just beneath the image of the titmouse. I wanted to say, in some formal way, why I found this work meaningful. Here are poems of transspecies collaboration. Here are poems involved in an ecosystem. Here are poems that take wing.)

The First 649 Days

The World Health Organization on Wednesday declared coronavirus a pandemic . . .

—*The Washington Post,* March 11, 2020

March 11, 2020

Today we entered lockdown. News of COVID has become more dire and direct: the first three cases in Ohio, the governor calling a state of emergency, the university suspending in-person instruction. This morning, K went on a massive grocery run to stock up for the next few weeks. We've charged about $800. We have beans, rice, apples, chips. We have boxes of food in the closet. As stockpilers, we're ahead of most folks in Athens and no doubt seem alarmist, but the situation in China and Italy looks gruesome. No reason to think it won't hit Athens. It's about when. We spent a long afternoon outside, liberating trees. We cut away the underbrush and briars from the sycamores and yanked down the grapevines that were choking out a cluster of oaks. Ro loved pulling down the vines. We also bought a chainsaw. We used it to clear the multi-stalked autumn olive and thornbushes, some as thick as small trees. Ro pointed to spots that needed to be chainsawed. There. And there. And there. He also set up a "camp" under the porch and made a catapult from a flyswatter.

March 16, 2020

"My heart is dancing, simply dancing," said Ro as we planned our day over breakfast. We took a family walk to the far side of the meadow. K showed us a spot where she likes to watch the grass blow in waves. Ro and I made forts in the bedroom with his stuffed animal, George. George is Peppa Pig's younger brother. I get to animate him. Ro wanted George to want to do everything Ro was doing, but he also wanted George not to be allowed to do those things. Ro also came up with a game called "Distraction." He pretends to work on his iPad, the way K and I work, and George tries to distract him. "Can I have a snack?" asked George. "You've already had three," said Ro. "How much longer are you going to work?" asked George. "Five and thirty minutes," said Ro. In the afternoon, we went outside to clear more brush. We set up Ro with various toys and games, but he wanted none of it. He needed to pee, to poop. He needed a snack. He had a question, another question. He felt kind of sad. Distractions. He then started doing things he knew he wasn't allowed to do: pulling up bits of rusty metal, sticking his fingers in the old fuse box and the HVAC unit. We finally had to confine him to a play area in the yard. He spent most of the time laying upside down on his red slide. "It's hard to be punished," he said. Later, he watched a concert by Red Yarn on Facebook Live. Red Yarn said, "If you ever feel scared, raise your hand." Ro raised his hand. "If you ever feel small, raise your hand." Ro raised his hand.

March 20, 2020

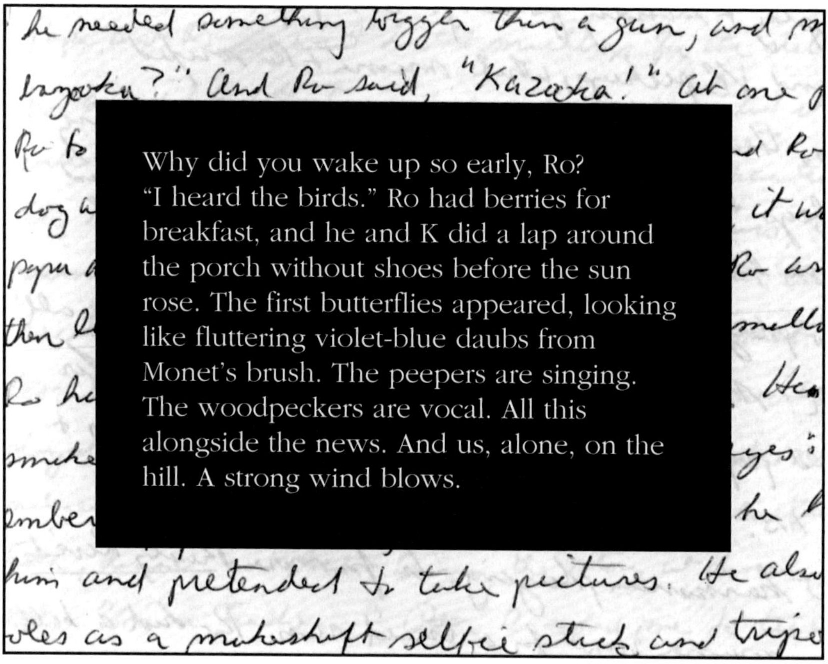

Why did you wake up so early, Ro?
"I heard the birds." Ro had berries for breakfast, and he and K did a lap around the porch without shoes before the sun rose. The first butterflies appeared, looking like fluttering violet-blue daubs from Monet's brush. The peepers are singing. The woodpeckers are vocal. All this alongside the news. And us, alone, on the hill. A strong wind blows.

April 1, 2020

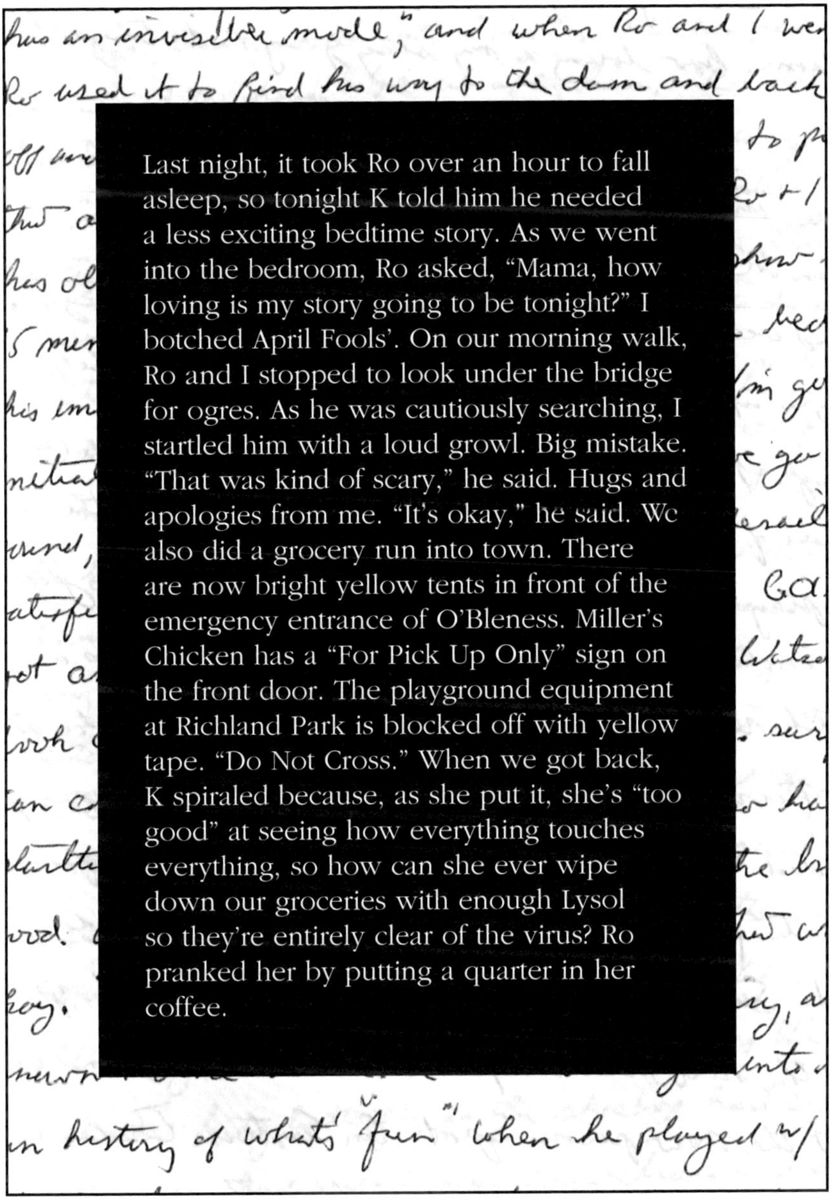

Last night, it took Ro over an hour to fall asleep, so tonight K told him he needed a less exciting bedtime story. As we went into the bedroom, Ro asked, "Mama, how loving is my story going to be tonight?" I botched April Fools'. On our morning walk, Ro and I stopped to look under the bridge for ogres. As he was cautiously searching, I startled him with a loud growl. Big mistake. "That was kind of scary," he said. Hugs and apologies from me. "It's okay," he said. We also did a grocery run into town. There are now bright yellow tents in front of the emergency entrance of O'Bleness. Miller's Chicken has a "For Pick Up Only" sign on the front door. The playground equipment at Richland Park is blocked off with yellow tape. "Do Not Cross." When we got back, K spiraled because, as she put it, she's "too good" at seeing how everything touches everything, so how can she ever wipe down our groceries with enough Lysol so they're entirely clear of the virus? Ro pranked her by putting a quarter in her coffee.

I remember how our days cycled

April 6, 2020

"Let's go up the hill and see if we can eat some redbud," suggested K. When we got to the blossoming trees, Ro pinched and nibbled. At one point, he went back to the house for his lawn chair so he could sit and snack. He said he'd also like his iPad. I said we might not want to eat all the blossoms that he could reach in one day. "Tomorrow," he said, "we can bring the stepstool." Ro had a rough moment with George. Ro wanted George to say that Ro's special pin was, in fact, George's special pin. When George said, "It's mine," Ro got very upset. I realized that Ro might not know what it means to be wrong, that is, that someone can say something—in this case loudly and forcefully and in a pig voice—and be wrong about what they're saying. So I explained being wrong. Ro lit up. "You're wrong, George! You're wrong!" Ro then wanted George and his other stuffies to be wrong, sometimes accidentally, sometimes on purpose.

into one continuous day

April 12, 2020

Ro awoke with a bump, falling out of bed and onto the floor. He immediately said, “I’m just panicking, because I’m so excited it’s Easter!” His Easter basket included candy, a light-up jump rope, a kite, and some long-desired fidget spinners. He wanted George to want it all. After breakfast, I walked across the field to the pine grove and hid. K and Ro followed. When Ro arrived, K and I surprised him with a “candy parade.” He’d walk down the path, and we’d toss candy into the air so it would rain down on him. George wanted all the candy, too. Later, the candy itself started speaking. “Orange,” for example, is the orange Starburst and speaks in a squeaky voice. “Snick,” the Snickers, is, as K says, “Crazy! He’s nuts, I tell you!” Over FaceTime, Ro said hello to Grammy Roo and Grampy Roo, as well as Gmaw and Gpaw. We all sang “Happy Birthday” to Gpaw, who turned eighty-one. He and Ro shared some celebratory ice cream on each side of the screen.

how time shifted from clocks and calendars

April 21, 2020

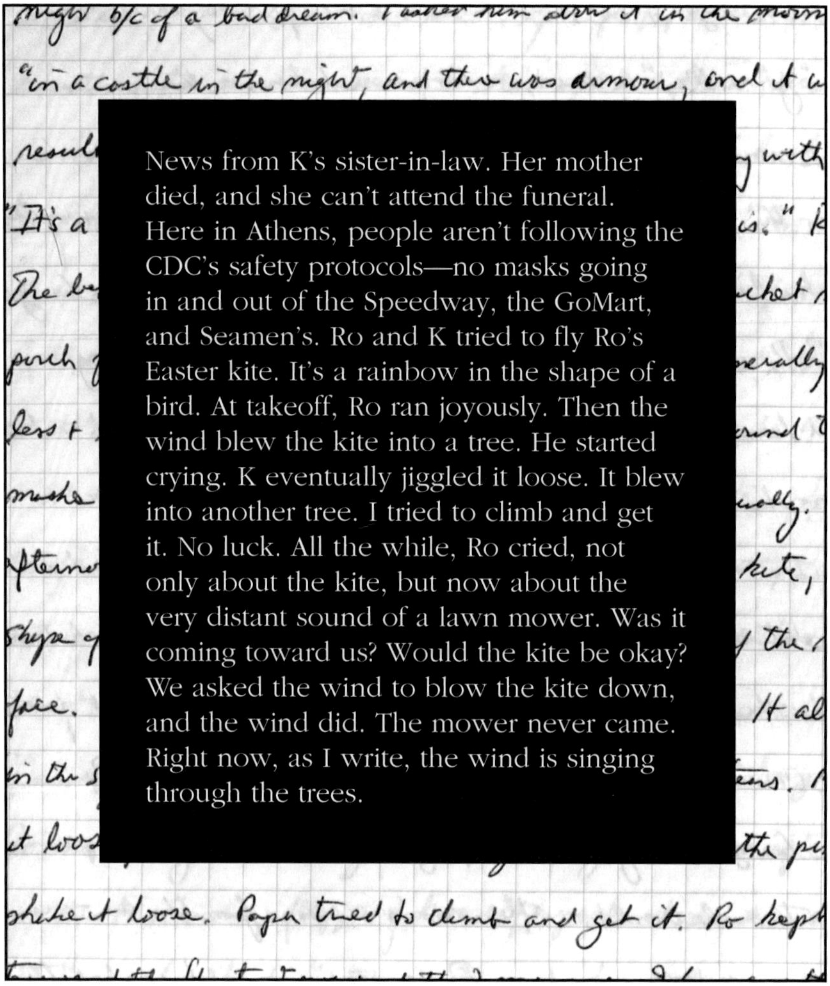

News from K's sister-in-law. Her mother died, and she can't attend the funeral. Here in Athens, people aren't following the CDC's safety protocols—no masks going in and out of the Speedway, the GoMart, and Seamen's. Ro and K tried to fly Ro's Easter kite. It's a rainbow in the shape of a bird. At takeoff, Ro ran joyously. Then the wind blew the kite into a tree. He started crying. K eventually jiggled it loose. It blew into another tree. I tried to climb and get it. No luck. All the while, Ro cried, not only about the kite, but now about the very distant sound of a lawn mower. Was it coming toward us? Would the kite be okay? We asked the wind to blow the kite down, and the wind did. The mower never came. Right now, as I write, the wind is singing through the trees.

to seasons, weather, the way spring broke

April 28, 2020

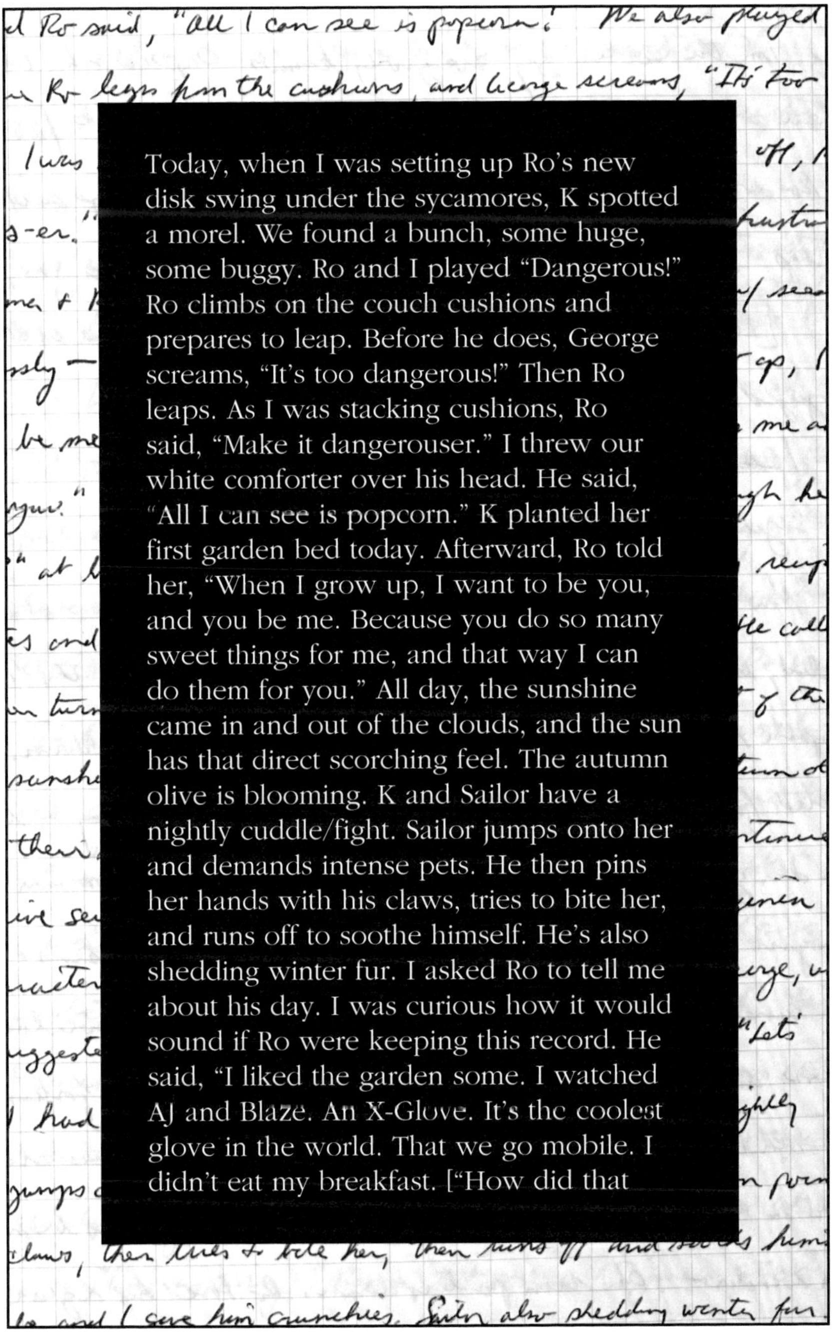

Today, when I was setting up Ro's new disk swing under the sycamores, K spotted a morel. We found a bunch, some huge, some buggy. Ro and I played "Dangerous!" Ro climbs on the couch cushions and prepares to leap. Before he does, George screams, "It's too dangerous!" Then Ro leaps. As I was stacking cushions, Ro said, "Make it dangerouser." I threw our white comforter over his head. He said, "All I can see is popcorn." K planted her first garden bed today. Afterward, Ro told her, "When I grow up, I want to be you, and you be me. Because you do so many sweet things for me, and that way I can do them for you." All day, the sunshine came in and out of the clouds, and the sun has that direct scorching feel. The autumn olive is blooming. K and Sailor have a nightly cuddle/fight. Sailor jumps onto her and demands intense pets. He then pins her hands with his claws, tries to bite her, and runs off to soothe himself. He's also shedding winter fur. I asked Ro to tell me about his day. I was curious how it would sound if Ro were keeping this record. He said, "I liked the garden some. I watched AJ and Blaze. An X-Glove. It's the coolest glove in the world. That we go mobile. I didn't eat my breakfast. ["How did that

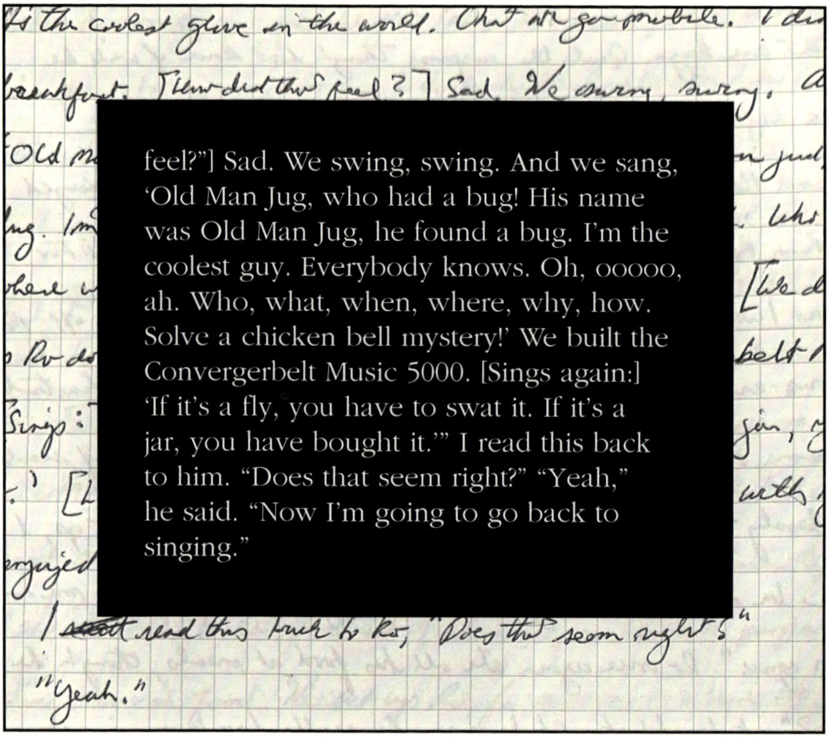

feel?"] Sad. We swing, swing. And we sang, 'Old Man Jug, who had a bug! His name was Old Man Jug, he found a bug. I'm the coolest guy. Everybody knows. Oh, ooooo, ah. Who, what, when, where, why, how. Solve a chicken bell mystery!' We built the Convergerbelt Music 5000. [Sings again:] 'If it's a fly, you have to swat it. If it's a jar, you have bought it.'" I read this back to him. "Does that seem right?" "Yeah," he said. "Now I'm going to go back to singing."

across the color-starved fields

May 2, 2020

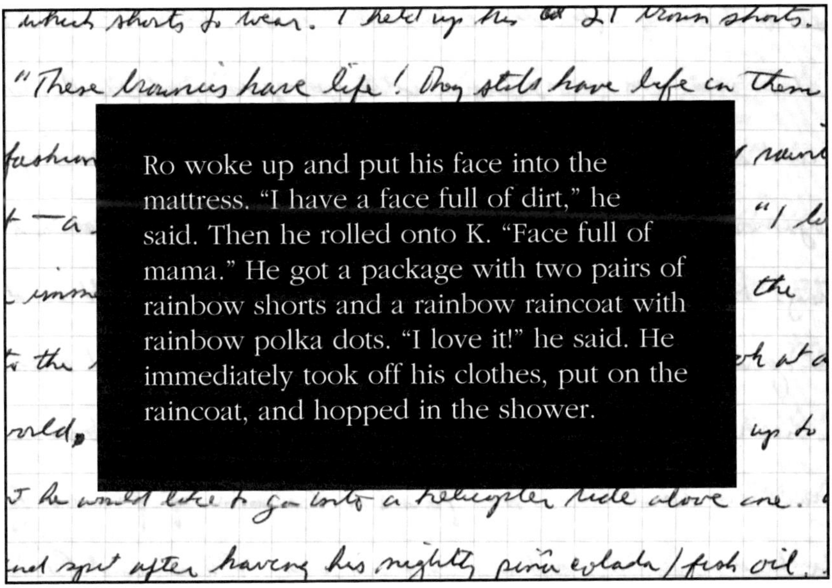

Ro woke up and put his face into the mattress. “I have a face full of dirt,” he said. Then he rolled onto K. “Face full of mama.” He got a package with two pairs of rainbow shorts and a rainbow raincoat with rainbow polka dots. “I love it!” he said. He immediately took off his clothes, put on the raincoat, and hopped in the shower.

in crocuses, bloodroot, and phlox.

May 10, 2020

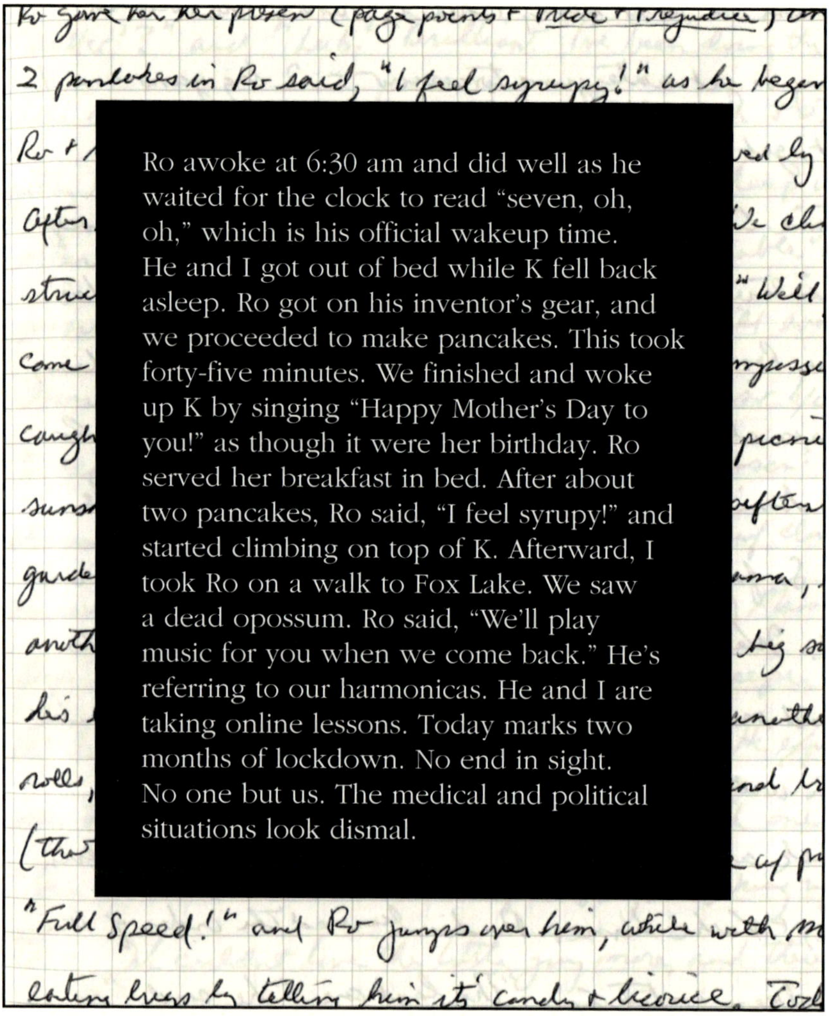

Ro awoke at 6:30 am and did well as he waited for the clock to read “seven, oh, oh,” which is his official wakeup time. He and I got out of bed while K fell back asleep. Ro got on his inventor’s gear, and we proceeded to make pancakes. This took forty-five minutes. We finished and woke up K by singing “Happy Mother’s Day to you!” as though it were her birthday. Ro served her breakfast in bed. After about two pancakes, Ro said, “I feel syrupy!” and started climbing on top of K. Afterward, I took Ro on a walk to Fox Lake. We saw a dead opossum. Ro said, “We’ll play music for you when we come back.” He’s referring to our harmonicas. He and I are taking online lessons. Today marks two months of lockdown. No end in sight. No one but us. The medical and political situations look dismal.

May 17, 2020

Ro woke up at 7:13 am and shouted, "It's past morning!" We played a good-morning tune for the sun. Ro has learned the order of the planets. "The last one," he said, "is Bluto, even though it's classified as a planetoid" (except for "Bluto," this is a line from *Peppa Pig*). One of our games involves Ro working under the "chassis" of our mattress, like it's a car. He'd shout out for tools, "Drill! Hammer! Ironing board!" I started teaching Ro to read. He's learned the *A* and *B* sounds. He even provides his own examples. He says, "Like 'batter' and 'lab'?" After each three-to-five-minute lesson, he gets a jellybean. On a walk with K, he found a four-leaf clover and Sailor "found" a bunny. Last night, Ro went to bed wearing his old sleeper with the hole in the toe. Later, he came out of the bedroom needing to pee and wearing his new penguin sleeper. "The blood in my toe wasn't flowing," he explained. "I can't remember which one." Then he remembered. "The thumb!" Ro occasionally says he misses going to Jolly Hoppers and gymnastics, and sometimes he seems to absorb our stress: the firings at the university, the furloughs, the state of Ohio unadvisedly opening back up. K spotted

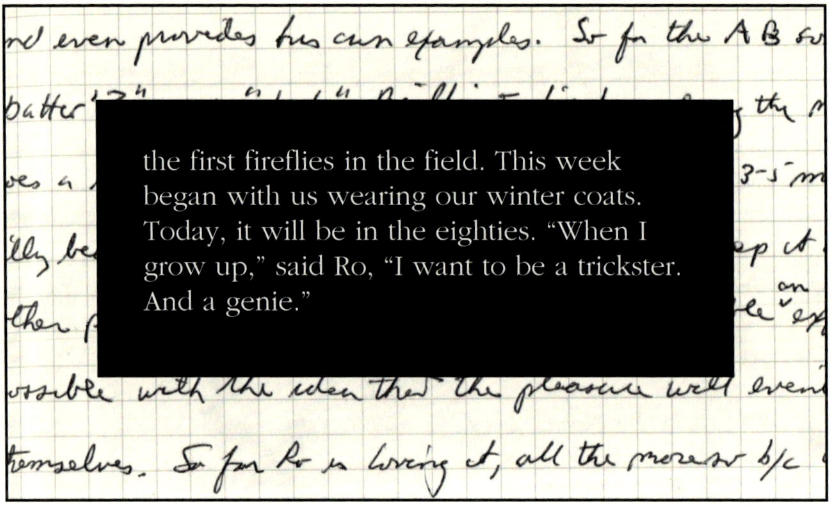

the first fireflies in the field. This week began with us wearing our winter coats. Today, it will be in the eighties. “When I grow up,” said Ro, “I want to be a trickster. And a genie.”

I remember grief like another skin

May 24, 2020

Yesterday was our hardest day of the pandemic so far, which, as the United States goes past 100,000 deaths, makes us fortunate. Ro woke up an hour before "seven, oh, oh," so we all had to wait it out. At his reading lesson, we played a game with coins. Ro pretended he didn't know the difference between a penny and a nickel. Not their difference in worth. He pretended he couldn't see a physical difference, that is, that one coin is clearly smaller and copper and the other coin is clearly silver and larger. Nope, they're the same. I thought I'd go mad. Then we did the weekly grocery run, which is a parking-lot pickup and always stressful, but with an additional stress: We stopped off to visit friends, and even though we were outside and in masks, they wouldn't keep their social distance. Add to this that once we got home and put away the groceries, K started stressing that the fridge wasn't cold enough, and her stress spread. Later, our neighbor came by and dropped off a few toys on the porch for Ro. Very sweet. However, he didn't tell K that his wife "isn't feeling well" until after they'd chatted for a while, and K didn't tell me until after I'd already blown up the giant inflatable

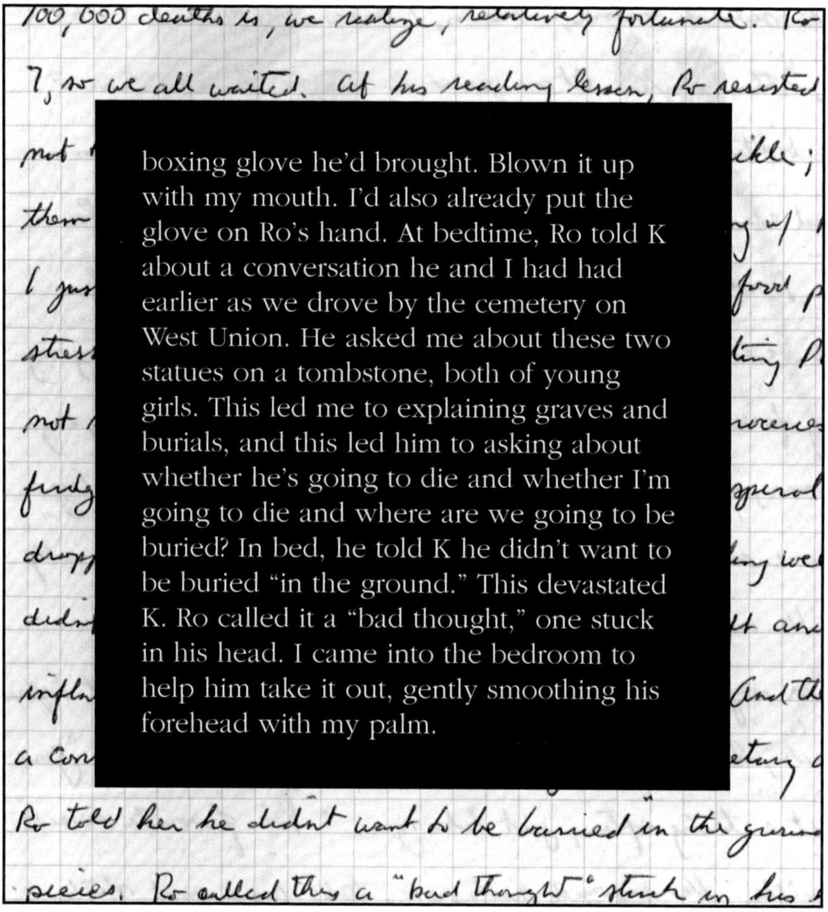

boxing glove he'd brought. Blown it up with my mouth. I'd also already put the glove on Ro's hand. At bedtime, Ro told K about a conversation he and I had had earlier as we drove by the cemetery on West Union. He asked me about these two statues on a tombstone, both of young girls. This led me to explaining graves and burials, and this led him to asking about whether he's going to die and whether I'm going to die and where are we going to be buried? In bed, he told K he didn't want to be buried "in the ground." This devastated K. Ro called it a "bad thought," one stuck in his head. I came into the bedroom to help him take it out, gently smoothing his forehead with my palm.

I couldn't shed.

May 31, 2020

Ro now reads entire sentences, such as "Stop the bot." He knows the letters *A, B, C, T, P, U,* and *O.* This morning, he wrote them all in sand with his finger. K started worrying that the eggs we bought last Saturday are rotten, so Ro got to throw them at some trees. He got a few good cracks. He still has bad thoughts. About one, he said, "I don't know what it is, but I know it's bad." We went to White's Mill and picked up some starters for yellow cherry tomatoes, patio snackers, and hot peppers.

June 7, 2020

Our pool arrived. K snagged one of the last ones on Amazon. We set it up around back by the sycamores. Ro has been splashing ferociously. He even started swim lessons, which has consisted of blowing bubbles (he's mixed about this), making big splashes as he kicks (he likes this), and walking around the pool while moving his arms like he's doing strokes (he make this into a race to beat/escape George). He's getting pink in the cheeks and tolerating K's extensive sunscreen routine. Today, K told him they're going to start speaking French together. "Bonjour! Je t'aime!" she said. "Namaste," he replied. I read more parenting advice from Janet Lansbury and decided to make it very clear to Ro that my job as his parent is to help him, especially when he's having a hard time. This hit. He now refers to it often. "Papa, will you help me?" "Papa, are you going to help me?" During our reading lesson, he sounded out "S U N." "Like the sun in the sky," I said. He corrected me, "In the solar system." I must have made a face, because he said, "I got that from *Bubble Guppies.*" Later, when we were playing with George, Ro wanted me to keep writing "B A D" on the Etch A

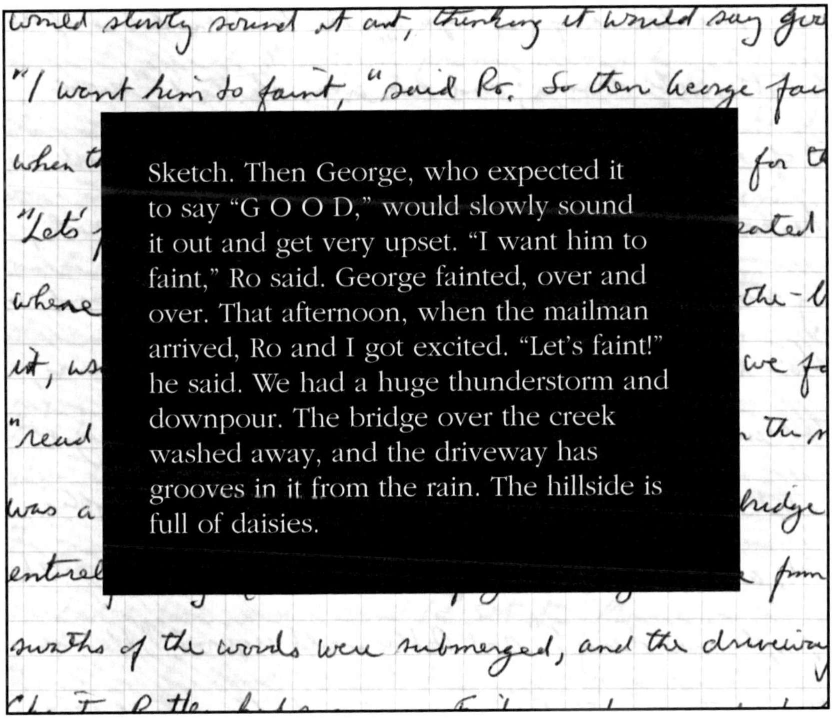

Sketch. Then George, who expected it to say "G O O D," would slowly sound it out and get very upset. "I want him to faint," Ro said. George fainted, over and over. That afternoon, when the mailman arrived, Ro and I got excited. "Let's faint!" he said. We had a huge thunderstorm and downpour. The bridge over the creek washed away, and the driveway has grooves in it from the rain. The hillside is full of daisies.

I remember aerial photos of mass graves

June 14, 2020

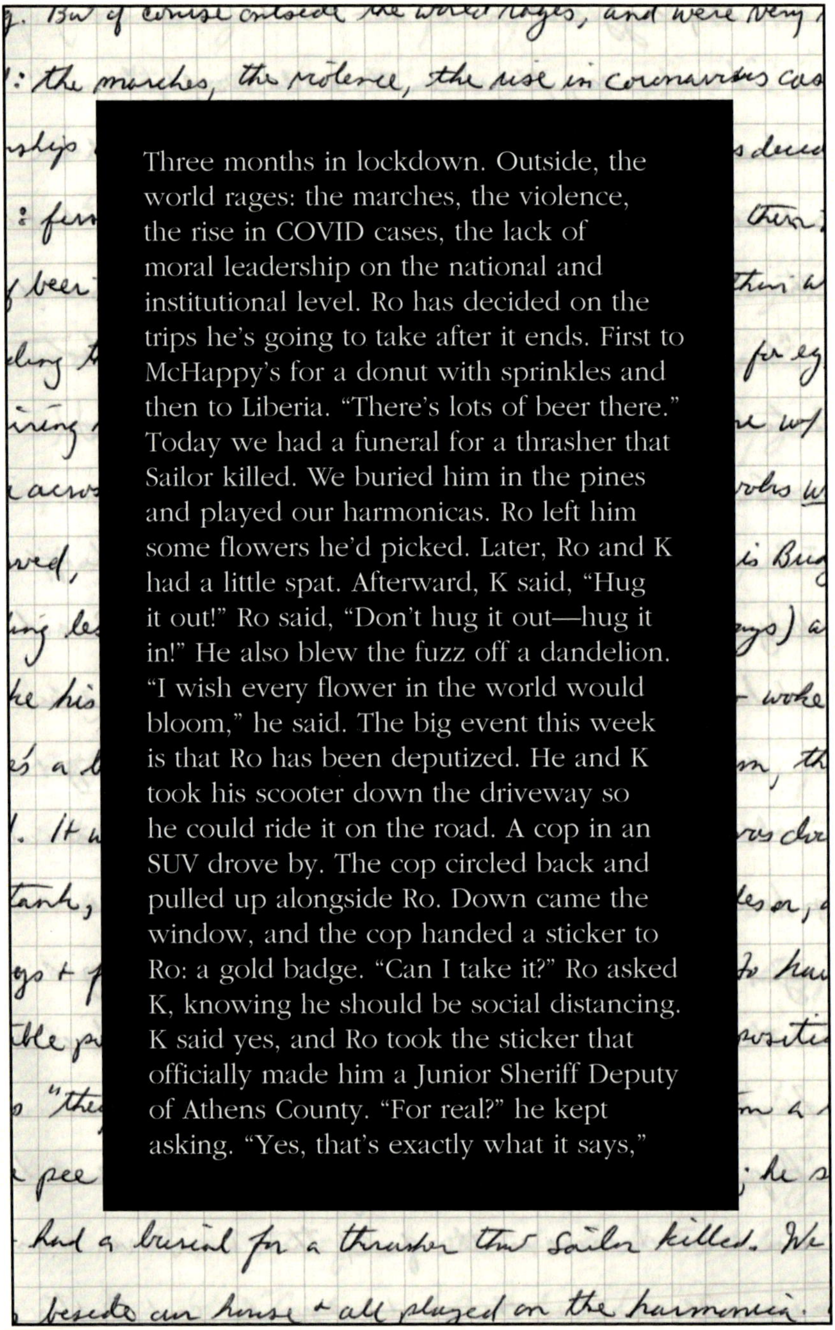

Three months in lockdown. Outside, the world rages: the marches, the violence, the rise in COVID cases, the lack of moral leadership on the national and institutional level. Ro has decided on the trips he's going to take after it ends. First to McHappy's for a donut with sprinkles and then to Liberia. "There's lots of beer there." Today we had a funeral for a thrasher that Sailor killed. We buried him in the pines and played our harmonicas. Ro left him some flowers he'd picked. Later, Ro and K had a little spat. Afterward, K said, "Hug it out!" Ro said, "Don't hug it out—hug it in!" He also blew the fuzz off a dandelion. "I wish every flower in the world would bloom," he said. The big event this week is that Ro has been deputized. He and K took his scooter down the driveway so he could ride it on the road. A cop in an SUV drove by. The cop circled back and pulled up alongside Ro. Down came the window, and the cop handed a sticker to Ro: a gold badge. "Can I take it?" Ro asked K, knowing he should be social distancing. K said yes, and Ro took the sticker that officially made him a Junior Sheriff Deputy of Athens County. "For real?" he kept asking. "Yes, that's exactly what it says,"

I'd say. When the cop drove off, he once again circled back and flashed his lights as he passed Ro. Whoa. Ro went home and stuck the badge onto a notebook. It's become his ticket book. He then declared that George was robbing our neighbor's house and sprinted out the door and up the hill to stop him. K ran after him. Ro called this his "sheriff speed." Then George started robbing our house, and Ro charged back home to stop him. Ever since, he's been sprinting around at "sheriff speed" and "deputy speed."

bodies wrapped in blankets, lying

June 22, 2020

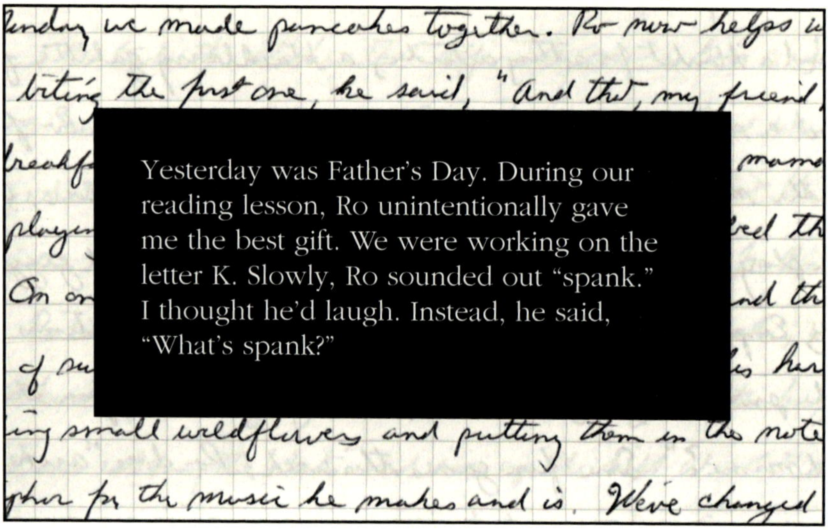

Yesterday was Father's Day. During our reading lesson, Ro unintentionally gave me the best gift. We were working on the letter K. Slowly, Ro sounded out "spank." I thought he'd laugh. Instead, he said, "What's spank?"

one next to the other next to the other.

June 28, 2020

We just had to blow-dry the footies on Ro's pajamas. He can't stand any wet spots, which is hard to avoid after three people take showers in a tiny bathroom. We usually end up changing his pajamas or his socks, sometimes the moment after we put them on. Tonight, he really wanted to wear his penguin onesie. No other pj's would do. Then the footies got wet. Cue the blow dryer. Ro started learning lowercase letters. It's confusing. Same sounds, but new symbols, particularly the *b* and *d*, which look so much alike. He and I made two books from scratch, folding and taping the paper together. He tells me the stories, I write them out, he illustrates them. Both of his stories climaxed in bad endings for George, including George being eaten by trolls. The wild blackcap berries are coming in. Ro hurries outside every morning with his bucket and picks every ripe berry. He has giant purple stains on his face and lips. Berry-purple fingers, too. Sailor got a tick on his butthole. Black-eyed Susans are in bloom.

July 5, 2020

Ro woke up and started dancing. Why? The Fourth of July means candy. He'd been anticipating another "candy parade," and that's what we did. We went back to the pine grove, and this time Ro got to decide, with each fistful of candy that went into the air and landed around him, that he was surprised. It was hot and humid. By the end, Ro felt too tired to pick up any candy. Instead, he asked us to do it. So K and I flung handfuls of candy at Ro, then picked it up from around his feet. We finished the day with a fire in the 90° heat. Ro ate two hotdogs and asked me to light and hold his sparklers for him. As for the candy, K and Ro have invented "Percy's Candy Emporium," where the candy gives Ro magical powers (gumdrops = invisibility, super-jumping, et cetera). Ro and I also played Candy Swing, Candy Gully, and Candy Volcano. In the pool, Ro got stung under the armpit by a bee. A Band-Aid and cream helped. "Once the sadness starts," Ro said, "it just never stops." A sadness started for K when she let the HVAC guy into the house without a mask. She's now living through COVID fears, and Ro and I are living through her living through them. Clearly, we're not ready to stop socially distancing, which is objectively the right

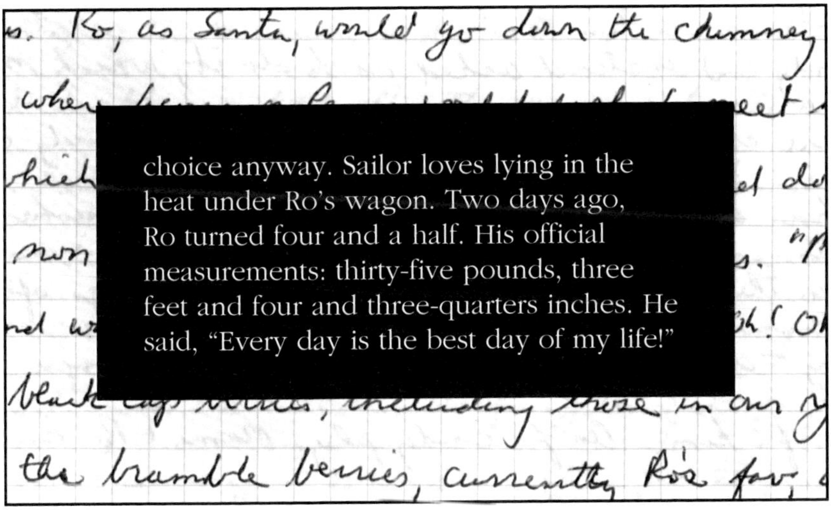

choice anyway. Sailor loves lying in the heat under Ro's wagon. Two days ago, Ro turned four and a half. His official measurements: thirty-five pounds, three feet and four and three-quarters inches. He said, "Every day is the best day of my life!"

I remember how the sky shuddered

July 12, 2020

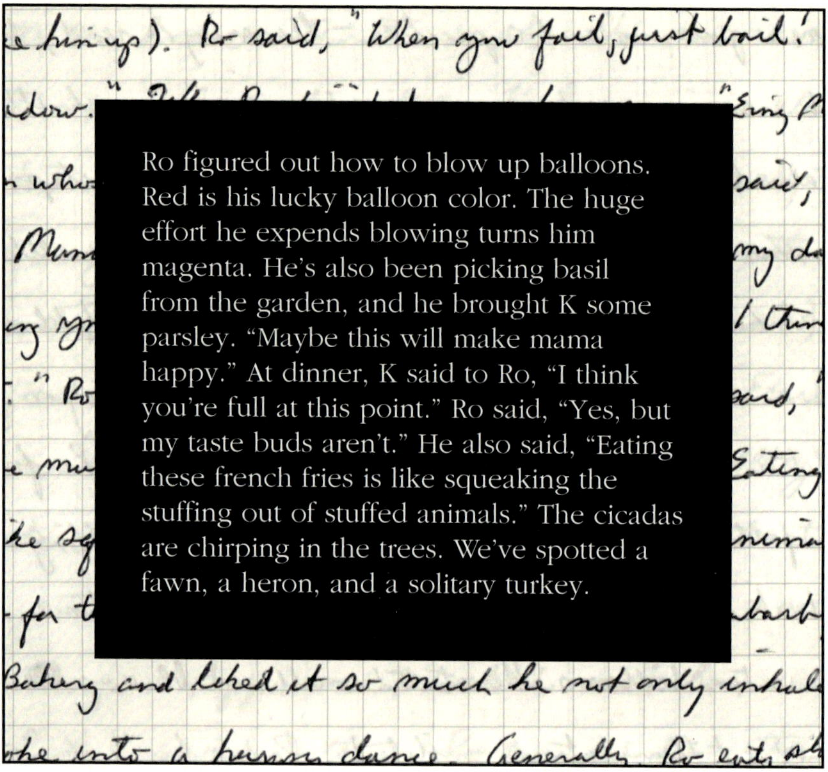

Ro figured out how to blow up balloons. Red is his lucky balloon color. The huge effort he expends blowing turns him magenta. He's also been picking basil from the garden, and he brought K some parsley. "Maybe this will make mama happy." At dinner, K said to Ro, "I think you're full at this point." Ro said, "Yes, but my taste buds aren't." He also said, "Eating these french fries is like squeaking the stuffing out of stuffed animals." The cicadas are chirping in the trees. We've spotted a fawn, a heron, and a solitary turkey.

when the medevac helicopters flew by

July 19, 2020

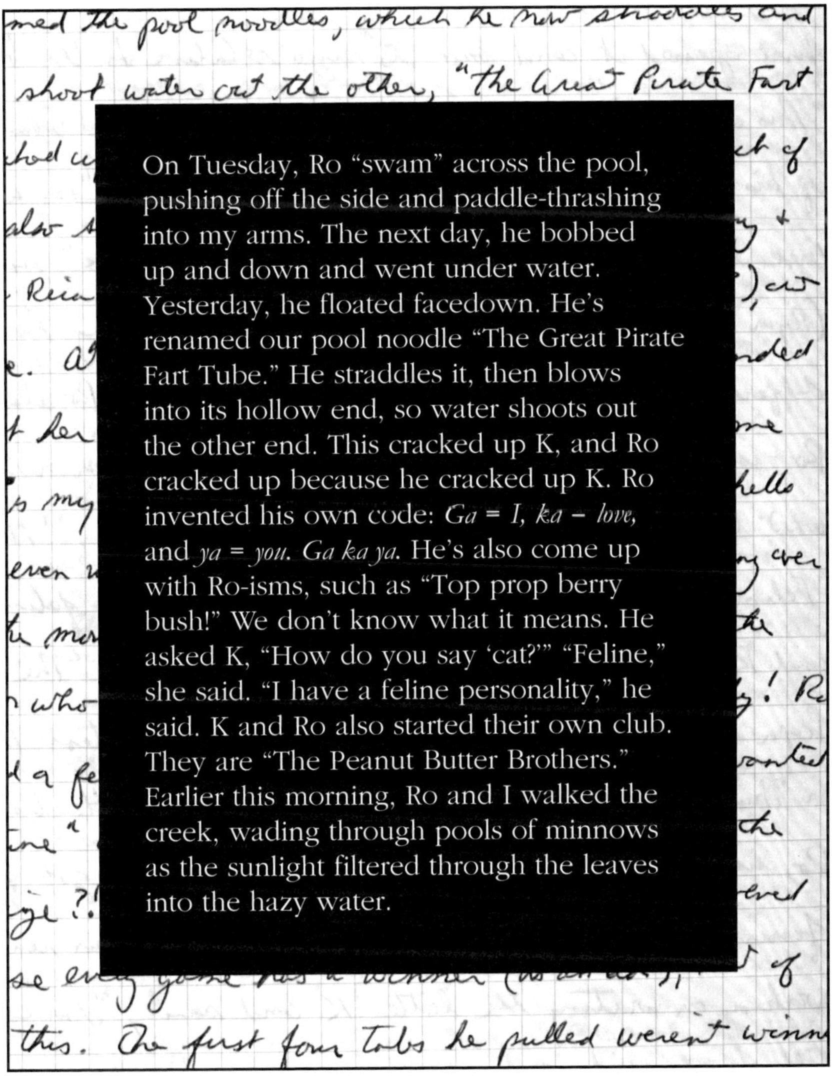

On Tuesday, Ro "swam" across the pool, pushing off the side and paddle-thrashing into my arms. The next day, he bobbed up and down and went under water. Yesterday, he floated facedown. He's renamed our pool noodle "The Great Pirate Fart Tube." He straddles it, then blows into its hollow end, so water shoots out the other end. This cracked up K, and Ro cracked up because he cracked up K. Ro invented his own code: *Ga = I, ka – love,* and *ya = you. Ga ka ya.* He's also come up with Ro-isms, such as "Top prop berry bush!" We don't know what it means. He asked K, "How do you say 'cat?'" "Feline," she said. "I have a feline personality," he said. K and Ro also started their own club. They are "The Peanut Butter Brothers." Earlier this morning, Ro and I walked the creek, wading through pools of minnows as the sunlight filtered through the leaves into the hazy water.

how we scrambled onto our porch

July 27, 2020

Ro had his first "taco night" (not on Tuesday). He and I browned ground beef. He and K prepped veggies. Then, at dinner, he made the tacos. His inaugural taco: one spoonful of meat, a few cherry tomatoes, shredded cheese, and crиme fraoche. "Would you make mine?" I asked. "I would be honored," he said. He also made K a "reverse taco," with cheese on the bottom and meat on top. As we raved about our tacos, he said, "I didn't know I had this talent. It was just stuck in me." The cherry tomatoes came from the garden. At first, Ro would eat every tomato before it had the chance to ripen—a little yellow was enough—but now so many of them are ripe there's enough for him to collect. K and Ro also planted a fall garden with peas and carrots and cucumbers. Earlier in the week, on a whim, I plopped Ro's jungle gym into the pool. He did all kinds of climbs and leaps. Our neighbor gave us a box of books, and we've been dipping into them. We started one based on an old folk tale. A fox drinks a milkmaid's milk. The milkmaid gets mad, takes a knife, and "cuts off the fox's tail." When I finished that line, I looked up and saw Ro was upset. Then tears. We tried to comfort him, quickly turning to the end of the story, where the fox gets his tail sewn back on. Nothing helped. Not until K declared we were going to throw away the book. "That book is done forever!" she shouted. Ro laughed, and K stuffed it in the garbage. The next morning Ro got up and, during his usual prebreakfast putter around the house, asked, "What was the big drama yesterday?" I said, "You got upset about a story." He said, "It's in the garbage." Today, on a walk at Fox Lake, he told me he wants to be a doctor. I asked him what kind. "For people, for animals?" He said, "For clouds."

to wave (*Hello!*) and wave (*We're here!*).

August 2, 2020

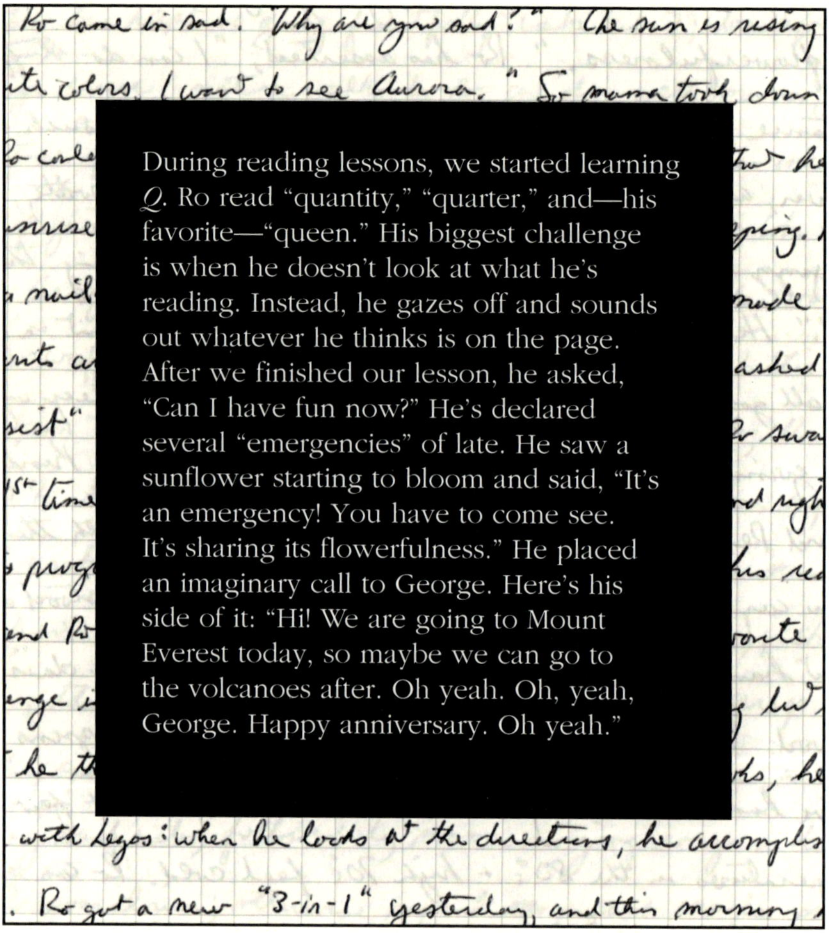

During reading lessons, we started learning *Q*. Ro read "quantity," "quarter," and—his favorite—"queen." His biggest challenge is when he doesn't look at what he's reading. Instead, he gazes off and sounds out whatever he thinks is on the page. After we finished our lesson, he asked, "Can I have fun now?" He's declared several "emergencies" of late. He saw a sunflower starting to bloom and said, "It's an emergency! You have to come see. It's sharing its flowerfulness." He placed an imaginary call to George. Here's his side of it: "Hi! We are going to Mount Everest today, so maybe we can go to the volcanoes after. Oh yeah. Oh, yeah, George. Happy anniversary. Oh yeah."

August 9, 2020

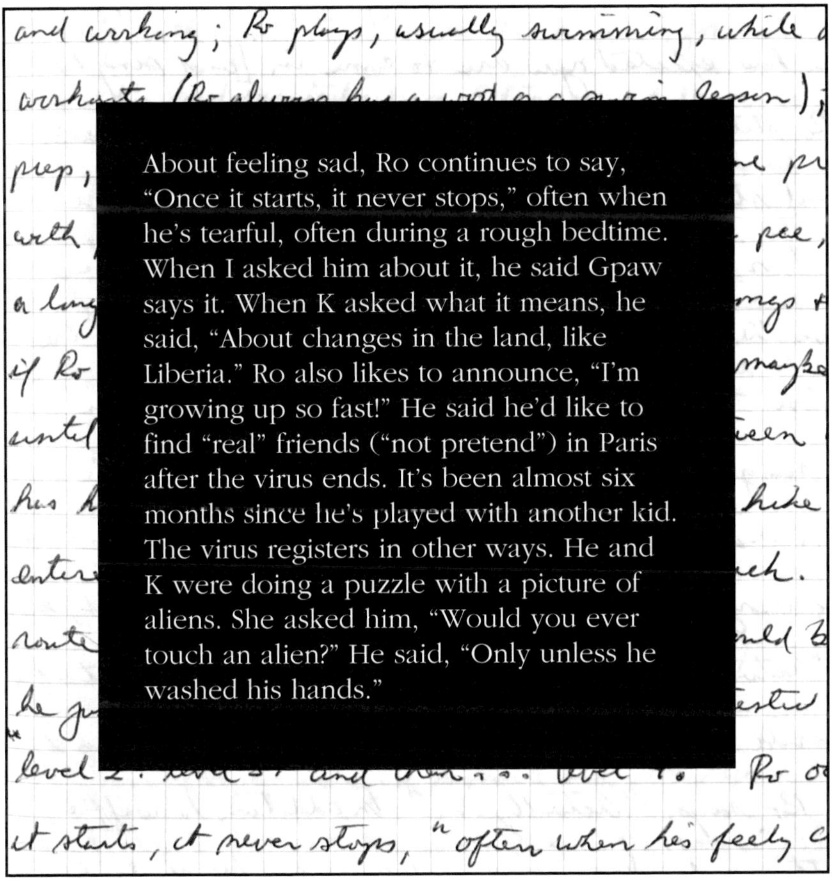

About feeling sad, Ro continues to say, "Once it starts, it never stops," often when he's tearful, often during a rough bedtime. When I asked him about it, he said Gpaw says it. When K asked what it means, he said, "About changes in the land, like Liberia." Ro also likes to announce, "I'm growing up so fast!" He said he'd like to find "real" friends ("not pretend") in Paris after the virus ends. It's been almost six months since he's played with another kid. The virus registers in other ways. He and K were doing a puzzle with a picture of aliens. She asked him, "Would you ever touch an alien?" He said, "Only unless he washed his hands."

I remember wondering how to make our life

August 16, 2020

Ro and I took Sailor to the vet. The entire drive, Sailor yowled in protest. Ro said he could speak cat and translated: "Sailor says he doesn't want to go." Our vet does "curbside drop off," so we handed over Sailor and strolled through the parking lot and looked at the storefronts. We peaked into a window that once was a cafй where we'd get cookies. Another COVID closing. Then we walked across the road and through the high weeds down to the riverbank. We watched the waterfall that runs next to White's Mill. Ro seems to have a green thumb. Another of his sunflowers blossomed, and he's currently growing a beanstalk. "Pruning tomatoes is like giving the plants a haircut," he said. He's also using conversational phrases like "Speaking of . . . " and "Is it my imagination, or . . . " He and K found a few last bramble berries, and he and I picked some sassafras. "It's good!"

amid so much death.

August 23, 2020

Tonight, as Ro was winding down for bed, he sai

Ro got very upset when we wouldn't order a Wild Kratt brothers superhero outfit for him. Later that night, he had "bad thoughts" about a scene from the show where the Kratt brothers go down into a sewer to look for discarded alligators. The bad thoughts lasted for over an hour and led to Ro suddenly trying to hit the bad thoughts out of his head. I stopped him and pulled him to me in a hug. "No, you can't do that," I said. "Okay," he said and quieted. I laid down, and he laid on my stomach. I slowly rubbed his back. He got heavier and heavier until he fell asleep. Ro also finds it hard when K gets angry about something, like whatever's happening for her at work. It makes him feel, in his word, "unsure." He also doesn't like when our lessons get tense, like when he doesn't look at the word that he's trying to copy and instead makes up the letters. He senses that I'm frustrated and rubs his stomach in a circle and breathes deeply. He also does this when he's worried about the virus, like when our neighbors stop by to chat on the porch, and we all struggle to keep a safe social distance. He rubs and he breathes. Other times, he feels bored or lonely or it feels to him like a slight when K and I work instead of play with him during his

his hikes — identifying trees and leaves, finding

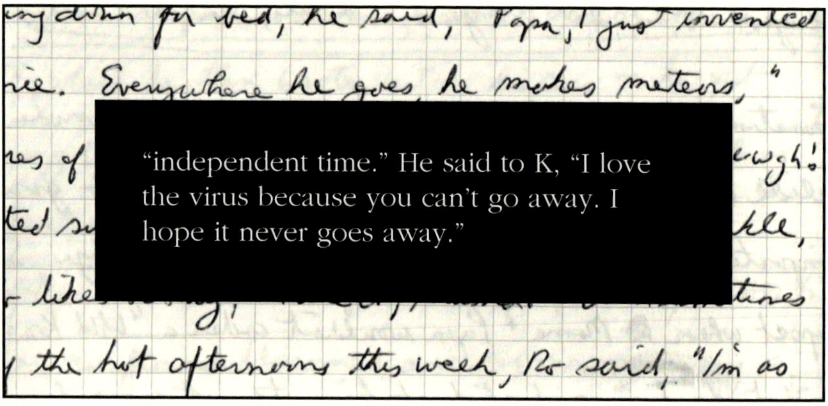

"independent time." He said to K, "I love the virus because you can't go away. I hope it never goes away."

August 30, 2020

This morning, when Ro and K went on a walk, Sailor followed them and suddenly bolted after a chipmunk. The chipmunk ran over Ro's boot. Then Sailor ran over Ro's boot. Sailor captured the chipmunk, then the chipmunk escaped. Neither K nor Ro know how badly Sailor mangled the chipmunk. (Sailor is fine.) Ro's "bad thoughts" continue. He's had some hard bedtimes, one with tears. The bad thoughts are often more like bad feelings. He doesn't want to share them because they're "too bad" or "too hard to say." Instead, he says, "It just keeps unraveling and unraveling!" and they're "coiled around each other in my belly." ("It will last forever!" he says. "It's useless!") Sometimes, he can start having bad thoughts about having bad thoughts. He's made up a motto, "Bad thoughts, bad thoughts, go away! Come again a grownup day!" It might also be the stresses of the pandemic. As I said to K, shouldn't we all be crying every day? K treated Ro with some essential oils. "Stress Away" and "Sleepy Eyes." He gets the giggles when she applies them. This morning he woke up and happily shouted, "It worked!" And then, "It can't last forever." We had one very cold swim, which resulted

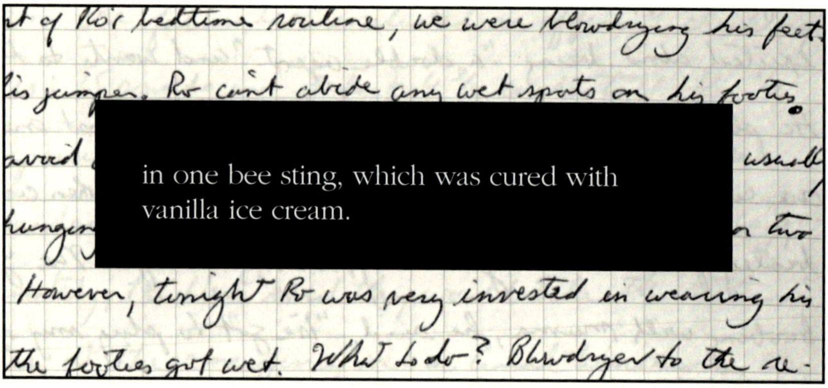

I remember dolphins in the Grand Canal

September 6, 2020

Tonight, we tried a new approach to "family dinner." Instead of rushing, we slowed down, built a fire, cooked hotdogs, munched potato chips. Ro roasted a marshmallow. Later, he ran around the fire, proclaiming he was the "kiss fairy" and giving us secret kisses on our backs. He's still having the same amorphous "bad thoughts." Here's how he describes them: "There's a family of bad thoughts. They dress up and put on plays in my head. Sometimes they dress up as things from long ago—before I can remember—big things that were extinguished by the meteor." K: "Like dinosaurs?" Ro: "Yes. And mountains with lava inside." K: "Volcanoes?" Ro: "Yes." One night, after I'd told Ro a bedtime story and K had gone into the bedroom to help him fall asleep, he came back out for a pee. "How's it going?" I asked. "So far it's going good." "That's great," I said. "Mama is really good at bedtime. She's been doing it your whole life." Ro: "Not you." "I'll try," I said, "but I'll never be as good as mama." Ro: "Ever." The big question he likes to ask now—and by "now," I mean at breakfast, at lunch, on walks, and in the car—is "What can I

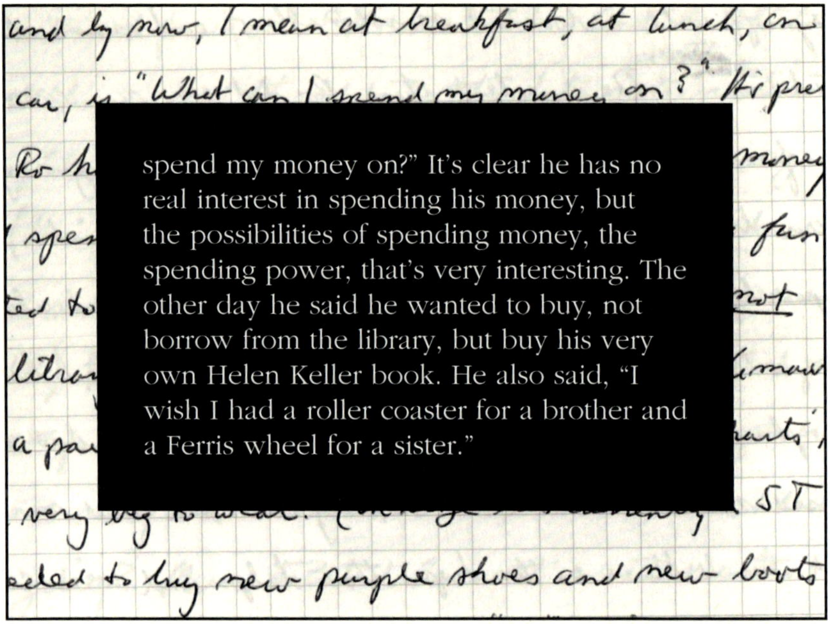

spend my money on?" It's clear he has no real interest in spending his money, but the possibilities of spending money, the spending power, that's very interesting. The other day he said he wanted to buy, not borrow from the library, but buy his very own Helen Keller book. He also said, "I wish I had a roller coaster for a brother and a Ferris wheel for a sister."

cresting above the cleaner, clearer water

September 13, 2020

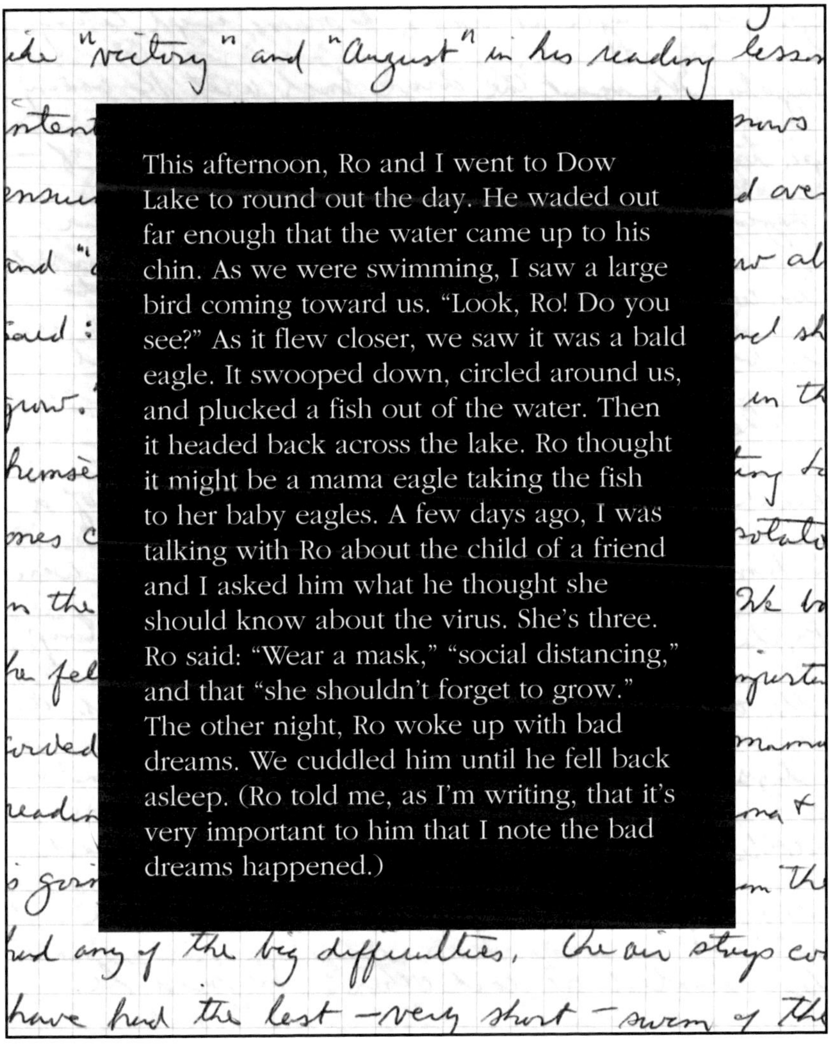

This afternoon, Ro and I went to Dow Lake to round out the day. He waded out far enough that the water came up to his chin. As we were swimming, I saw a large bird coming toward us. "Look, Ro! Do you see?" As it flew closer, we saw it was a bald eagle. It swooped down, circled around us, and plucked a fish out of the water. Then it headed back across the lake. Ro thought it might be a mama eagle taking the fish to her baby eagles. A few days ago, I was talking with Ro about the child of a friend and I asked him what he thought she should know about the virus. She's three. Ro said: "Wear a mask," "social distancing," and that "she shouldn't forget to grow." The other night, Ro woke up with bad dreams. We cuddled him until he fell back asleep. (Ro told me, as I'm writing, that it's very important to him that I note the bad dreams happened.)

how the earth thrived without us.

September 20, 2020

K taught Ro how to finger-knit. He's already knit two green scarves. He got upset when he and K had to stop for lunch. Here are some things Ro said on a walk with K. She texted them to me: "I'm blue." "I feel down in the dumps." "I feel awful." "This day is full of stuff I don't want to do." "I feel heartbroken." "This is the worst day of my life." "I want to do something out of the ordinary." "I feel a little reckless." All on one walk. Ro did enjoy taking down the swimming pool. We emptied it yesterday, and Ro marched around in the draining water. His pants got very wet. Sailor likes when we have picnics and makes his presence known whenever there's meat, especially fish.

September 28, 2020

Ro started his second week of kindergarten-at-home. As I write, he and K are tasting applesauce they made this morning. Ro describes it as "cinnamony" and "apple-y," which are indeed the only two ingredients. Kindergarten started with Ro in high spirits. Last Monday, he awoke to new educational posters on the walls and the present of a "wonder journal." The high didn't last. He quickly realized kindergarten meant reading, numbers, crafts, and walks. By the end of the first day, he had tears. "It's not quite as fun as you thought, is it, buddy? "Yeah," he said, "it's not like a carnival." It did get better. Ro read *Max and Mo Go Apple Picking* all by himself. He dissected apples. He made apple trees out of pipe cleaners and beads. (Apples are our theme.) On Friday, we drove north toward Zanesville to visit an apple orchard. It was idyllic, partially an orchard, partially a Zen garden. It was also Trump country, where no one wore masks. Ro got to cross arched bridges, find his way through patches of bamboo trees, climb into a treehouse and go down a slide, feed carp in a koi pond, pee surreptitiously alongside K behind some bushes, climb a lookout tower, and pick dozens of apples. His favorites are the

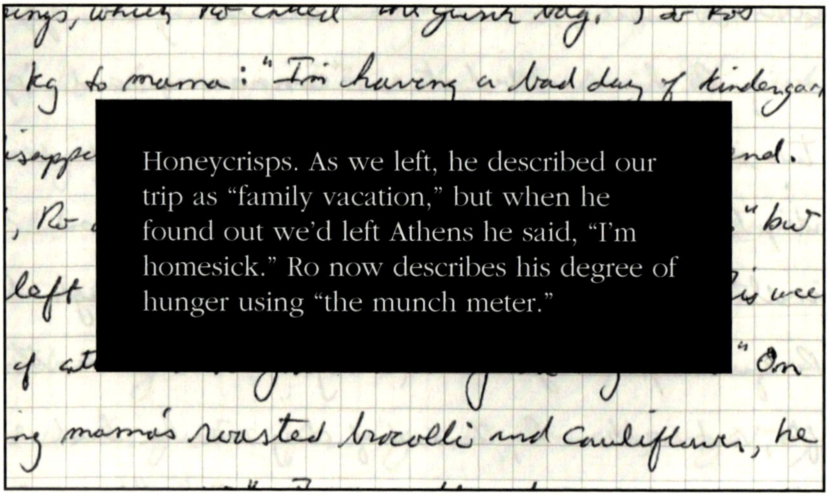

Honeycrisps. As we left, he described our trip as “family vacation,” but when he found out we’d left Athens he said, “I’m homesick.” Ro now describes his degree of hunger using “the munch meter.”

I remember thinking, *This is your childhood*

October 4, 2020

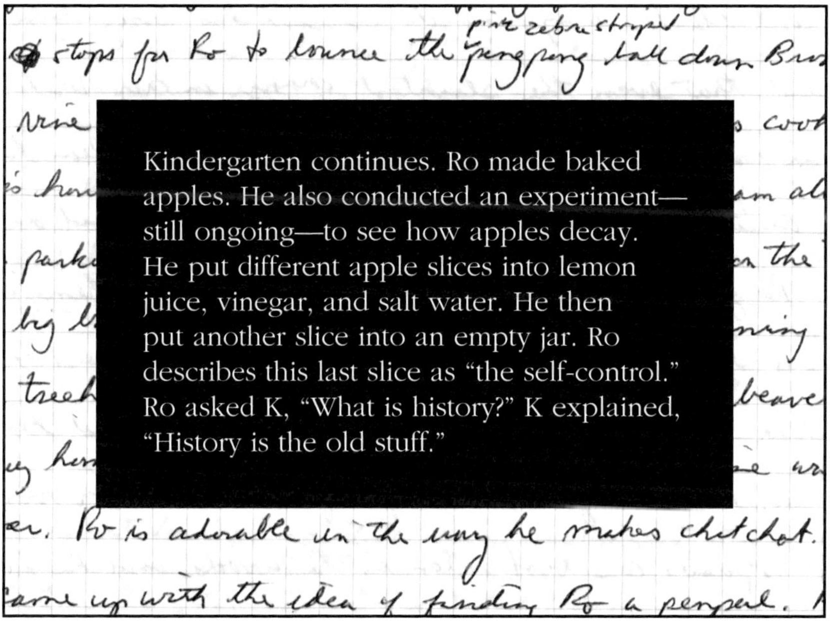

Kindergarten continues. Ro made baked apples. He also conducted an experiment—still ongoing—to see how apples decay. He put different apple slices into lemon juice, vinegar, and salt water. He then put another slice into an empty jar. Ro describes this last slice as "the self-control." Ro asked K, "What is history?" K explained, "History is the old stuff."

October 11, 2020

Today marks the eighth month of lockdown. Ro can now more or less put on his mask by himself and "visit" outside with others. He also brings up the virus "rules." At lunch, he said, "We're allowed to touch." K and I affirmed, yes, we're allowed touch one another in our family. K came the closest yet to a COVID scare. She and her friend had gone on a walk, and the next day her friend let her know she'd come down with a sore throat and was getting a COVID test. This meant three days of anxiety, if not for K's friend, then for K and the rest of us. The test was negative. Despite this, K remains worried because she hasn't had an appetite since last night. (She did manage to eat both breakfast and lunch today.) Today, I also got a drive-through COVID test at a building behind the fairgrounds. It's for my appointment at the James Center in a few days. The nurse walked up. I rolled down my window and tilted my head back. She swabbed, I winced, and she said, "That's it." Ro has been saying phrases from his shows, like "Oh, shucks!" "Aw nuts!" and "I give up!" We started a new theme for kindergarten: leaves. Ro made a "stained-glass window" by sticking different colored leaves on

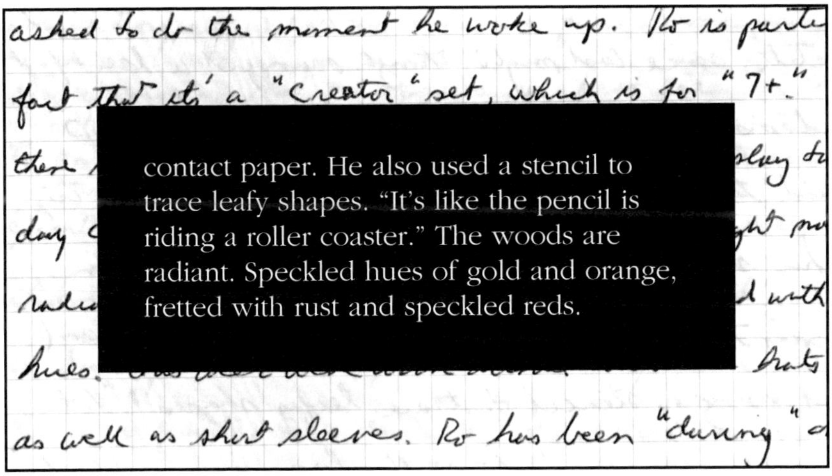

contact paper. He also used a stencil to trace leafy shapes. "It's like the pencil is riding a roller coaster." The woods are radiant. Speckled hues of gold and orange, fretted with rust and speckled reds.

that these were the only days

October 18, 2020

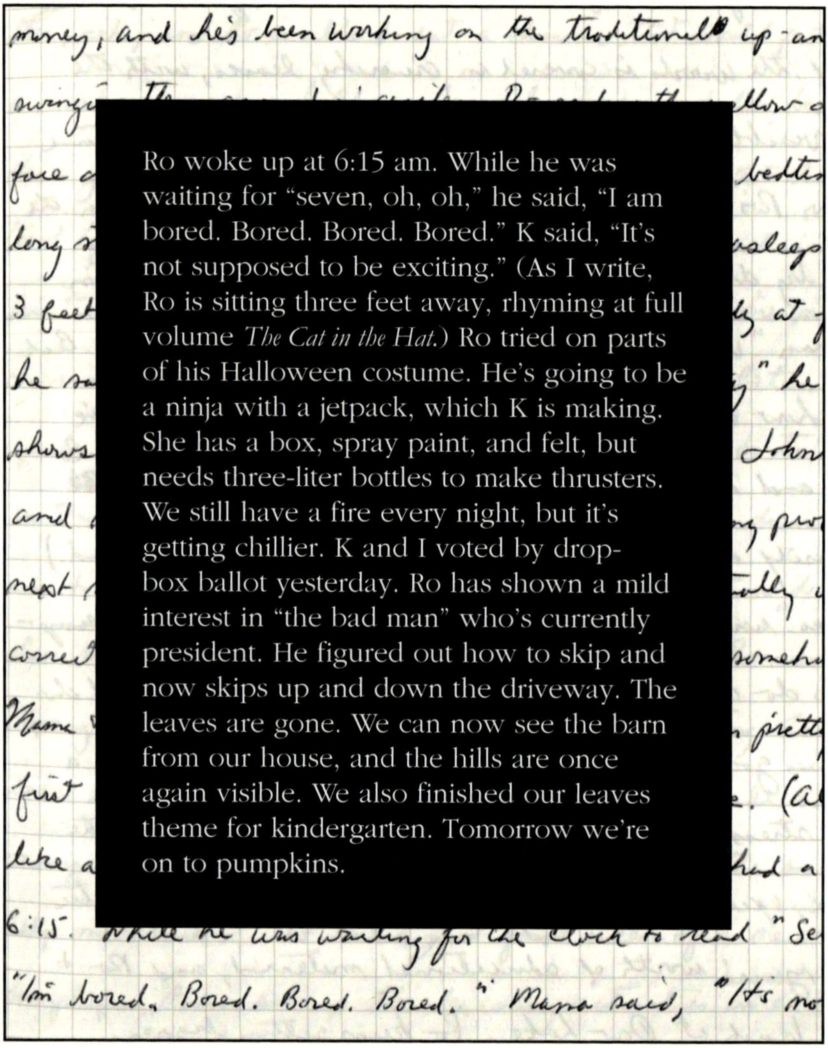

Ro woke up at 6:15 am. While he was waiting for "seven, oh, oh," he said, "I am bored. Bored. Bored. Bored." K said, "It's not supposed to be exciting." (As I write, Ro is sitting three feet away, rhyming at full volume *The Cat in the Hat.*) Ro tried on parts of his Halloween costume. He's going to be a ninja with a jetpack, which K is making. She has a box, spray paint, and felt, but needs three-liter bottles to make thrusters. We still have a fire every night, but it's getting chillier. K and I voted by drop-box ballot yesterday. Ro has shown a mild interest in "the bad man" who's currently president. He figured out how to skip and now skips up and down the driveway. The leaves are gone. We can now see the barn from our house, and the hills are once again visible. We also finished our leaves theme for kindergarten. Tomorrow we're on to pumpkins.

you'd ever be four, then five.

October 25, 2020

The bottles are the base for the jet pack. Mama has spra

Yesterday, Ro tried Coke for the first time. We brought home three three-liter bottles for his jetpack. K spraypainted them black and cut out felt "fire" to shoot from their spouts. As we were dumping out the Coke, we poured a little for Ro. He drank it and shrieked, then staggered backward, clutching the cup to his chest. He was clearly experiencing a caffeine-and-sugar jolt, somewhere beyond pleasure. Ro can eat a dinner that would put a trucker to shame: one and a half pulled-pork sandwiches, a big pile of chips, baked beans, red peppers, and cucumbers. He still takes his time eating—we still need to set a timer—and he flips upside down between bites. In fact, flipping is now his favorite way to travel in the car whenever he doesn't have to wear a seatbelt, like when we take down the garbage or drive to the Fox Lake parking lot, where he gets to steer the car in donuts. The other day, I was pushing him in the swing, and he said, "Trees really help me think." For our new kindergarten theme, K set up Ro's learning activities in a bunch of white paper bags and put them under Ro's desk. When he woke up, it was like a learning version of Christmas. The big hit was his own real

bakes him cookies. The other day — a beautiful fall d

orange leaves falling — as I was pushing Ro in the sw

hammer with a shortened grip. He used it to hammer golf tees into a pumpkin. He also roasted pumpkin seeds and learned how to count them by twos and tens. 570 seeds total. Sailor killed a rabbit larger than he is and gnawed on it all day. We kept him outside, figuring he'd barf. And what did we find the next morning when we went upstairs, gooped and piled high on the couch? Ro and K shrieked at the sight of it. (I cleaned it up.) As Halloween approaches, Ro reminded us of the Pete the Cat line, "You've got to be scared to be brave." We asked him what K and I should be. "Mr. and Mrs. Laundry Basket."

November 1, 2020

On Halloween morning, Ro found a pumpkin he named "Pumpky" full of candy, waiting for him on the couch. He told us his first original ghost story: "The vampire wanted to try the candy corn, but it didn't taste bloody enough, so he added 10,000 gallons of blood. Then threw up. The end." In the evening, we put a freshly carved pumpkin, with a new vampire smile, in the window and walked up to the top of the hill in the twilight to see it flicker. The other day while Ro was taking a bath and K was singing to him, he asked, "Is this a Jesus song? Who is Jesus?" Also, "Will I live forever?" K said, "That's what Gmaw and Gpaw would say." "It's a complicated question," he said. "I am blown away." He also said to K, "Playing with you is the number one goal of my life." During a night walk, Ro repeatedly made wishes on every star, one after another, repeatedly singing, "Star light, star bright, first star I see tonight . . . " as though he hadn't already seen or wished on any of the previous stars. The wind has blown so hard there's a tree down behind our house, another across the driveway, and another across Brown Road.

I remember the multiflora rose

November 8, 2020

Ro and I had an adventure on the ROTC course up at the Ridges. He walked across several huge balance beams made from logs, played on a large wooden teeter-totter, swung on ropes, and ran fast. Afterward, he said, "I am cooked." We took a shortcut straight down one of the huge hills and slid and slipped our way back to the car. Ro immediately peeled off his clothes: shirt! shoes! socks! Driving out, I saw what looked like a deer trapped inside a utility fence. I stopped and turned on the hazards. Ro got redressed. As we neared the fence, we saw a doe lying on her side. She wasn't trapped, but she didn't get up. Nearby, we spotted a buck, probably a few years old judging from his horns. He kept watching us, but also didn't move. We wondered if maybe the doe was hurt. Ro thought he might climb the fence and help but, as he later told K, he worried "the buck might charge." I noticed the doe looked very round. Maybe she was giving birth? We looked up some images of deer in labor. Sure enough. We gently backed away. At the car, Ro re-stripped, and we headed home. Last night, I made up a bedtime story with the aim of lulling Ro to sleep. It was about three turtles crossing a creek. Then a fox comes along and

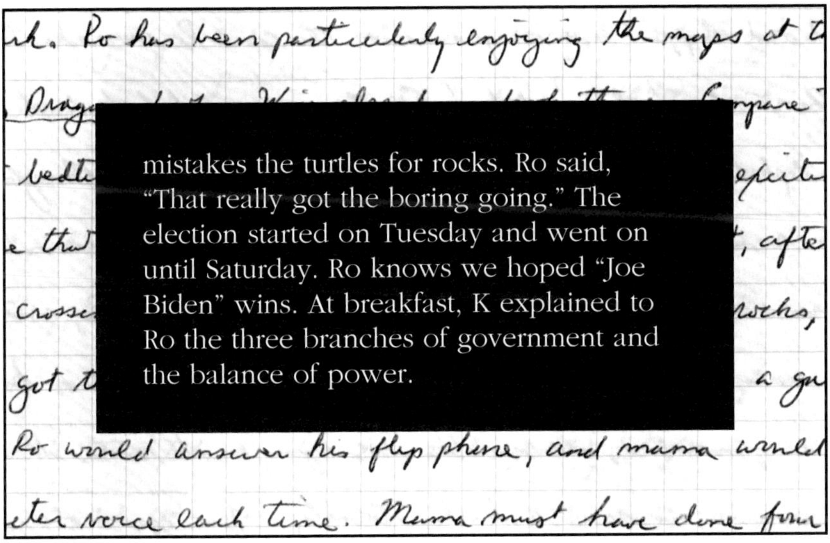

mistakes the turtles for rocks. Ro said, "That really got the boring going." The election started on Tuesday and went on until Saturday. Ro knows we hoped "Joe Biden" wins. At breakfast, K explained to Ro the three branches of government and the balance of power.

reaching across the empty trails

November 16, 2020

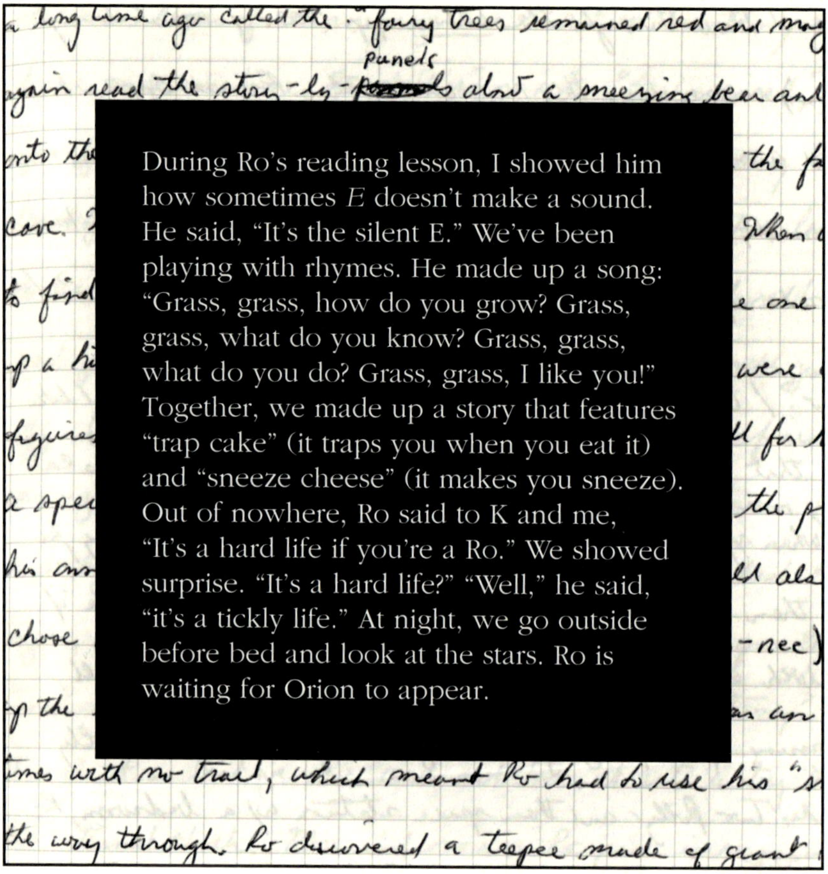

During Ro's reading lesson, I showed him how sometimes *E* doesn't make a sound. He said, "It's the silent E." We've been playing with rhymes. He made up a song: "Grass, grass, how do you grow? Grass, grass, what do you know? Grass, grass, what do you do? Grass, grass, I like you!" Together, we made up a story that features "trap cake" (it traps you when you eat it) and "sneeze cheese" (it makes you sneeze). Out of nowhere, Ro said to K and me, "It's a hard life if you're a Ro." We showed surprise. "It's a hard life?" "Well," he said, "it's a tickly life." At night, we go outside before bed and look at the stars. Ro is waiting for Orion to appear.

entangling itself, thicker and thicker.

November 22, 2020

We're still setting Ro's meal alarm. Sometimes, right before it goes off, he'll jump into "turbo speed," gasping and eating huge spoonfuls of yogurt. Other times, nah. Today, he managed to "finish" lunch only because K jammed four pieces of his avocado into her mouth at the final moment. Is this the opposite of a growth spurt? Is this a revolt against pandemic overparenting? It's also clear that Ro's internal clock, like K's, isn't rushed. Usually, he'll discover six or seven steps between "Please put on your socks" and his socks going on, including the sudden need to change all of his other clothes. When we're chatting as a family, Ro alerts us if K or I have talked too long by saying, "You interrupted me." We apologize and ask what he'd like to say. In most cases, he doesn't have anything to say. So, he improvises, "I just wanted to say you're the best papa in the whole world." Ro has figured out how these sorts of sweet words affect us. (K, for example, has requested I record here that Ro said, "Mama, you're my home star.") The first snow fell for a few minutes. Gmaw and Gpaw sent Ro a package, which the FedEx guy left down at the road by the garbage. It got stolen. Sadness all around. K and Ro are outside

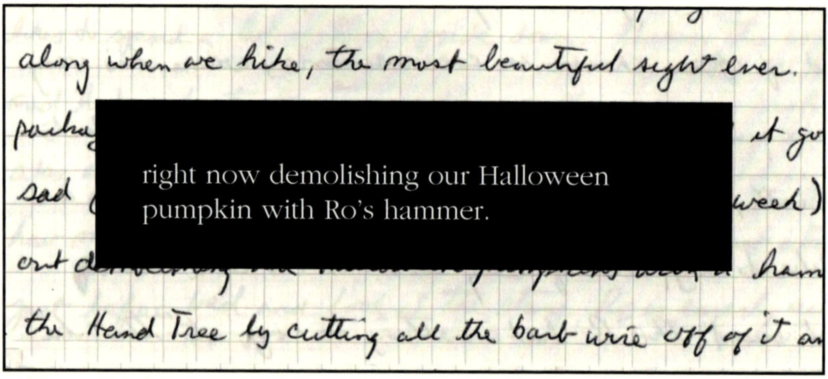
along when we hike, the most beautiful sight ever.
right now demolishing our Halloween
pumpkin with Ro's hammer.
the Hand Tree by cutting all the barb-wire off of it an

November 29, 2020

We went to White's Mill and picked out our Christmas tree. We hit on the idea at breakfast, and Ro and K immediately started shrieking, so much so that Ro got carried away and bit K. We once again have a Fraser fir. We put it upstairs by the big windows that overlook the fields and woods. This put us fully in Christmas mode: K played carols to and from White's Mill, and Ro is ready to start his Advent calendar on Tuesday. Back on Thursday, however, we were in full Thanksgiving mode. When I got up, the trees along the hillside were full of turkey vultures, roosting, spreading their wings, shuttling and soaring over the hilltop. Appalachian Gothic. K and Ro were still asleep at 8:00 am, so I let Sailor wake them up. Sailor curled up at the head of the bed. Ro rolled over and cuddled Sailor, thinking he was K, then woke up. Surprise! Ro helped K prep the turkey, and later we feasted on turkey, stuffing, wild rice, creamed greens, rolls, and gravy. Afterward, we started watching *The Secret Lives of Pets.* Ro loved the opening, but then two of the dogs started fighting. He got up and walked away before K and I knew what was happening. Later, he used the term *bump* to explain how watching scenes like that

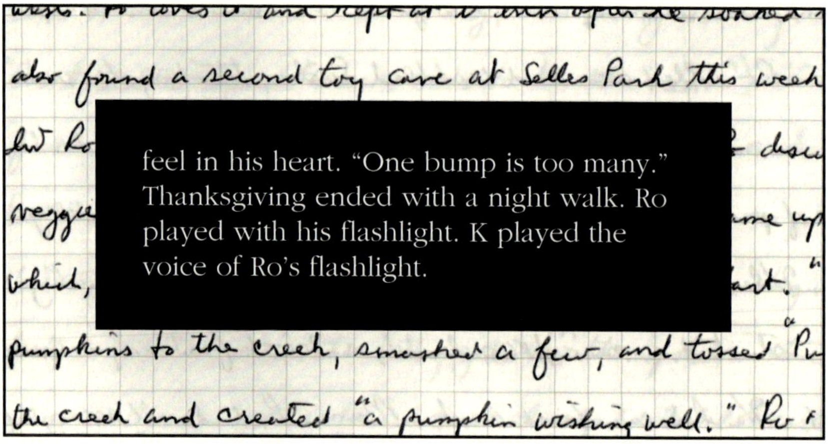

feel in his heart. “One bump is too many.” Thanksgiving ended with a night walk. Ro played with his flashlight. K played the voice of Ro’s flashlight.

December 7, 2020

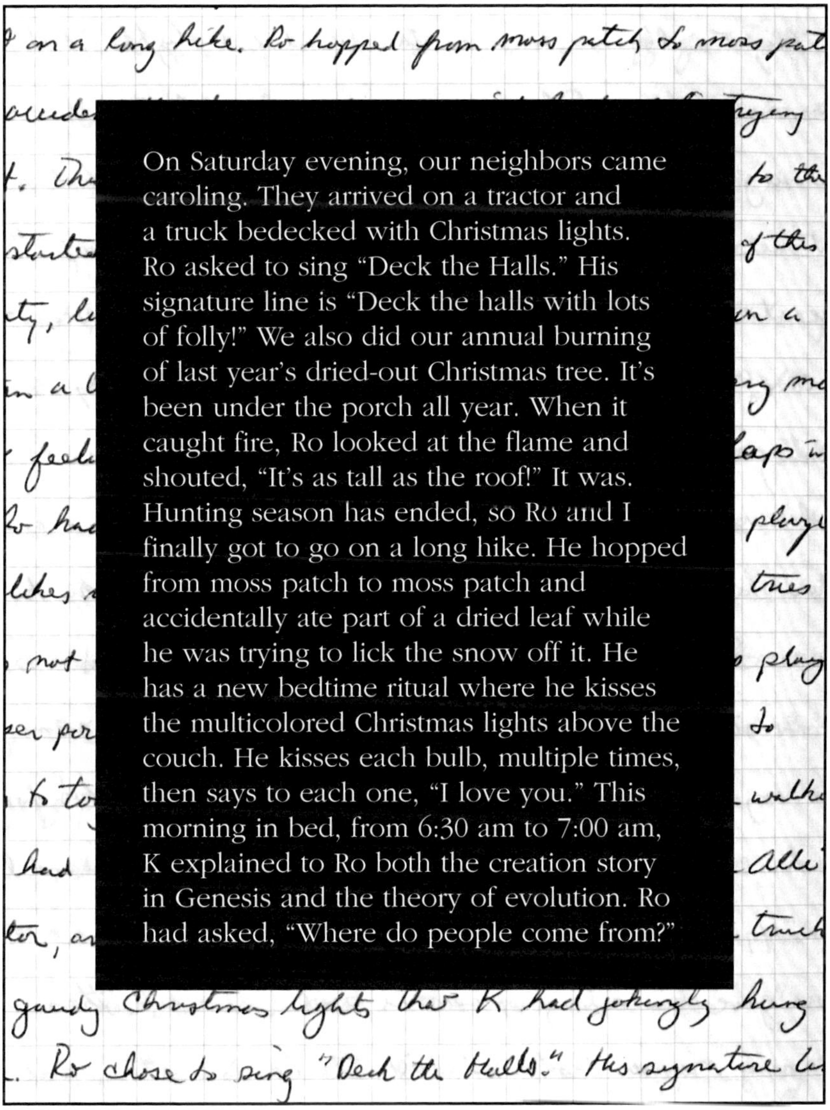

On Saturday evening, our neighbors came caroling. They arrived on a tractor and a truck bedecked with Christmas lights. Ro asked to sing "Deck the Halls." His signature line is "Deck the halls with lots of folly!" We also did our annual burning of last year's dried-out Christmas tree. It's been under the porch all year. When it caught fire, Ro looked at the flame and shouted, "It's as tall as the roof!" It was. Hunting season has ended, so Ro and I finally got to go on a long hike. He hopped from moss patch to moss patch and accidentally ate part of a dried leaf while he was trying to lick the snow off it. He has a new bedtime ritual where he kisses the multicolored Christmas lights above the couch. He kisses each bulb, multiple times, then says to each one, "I love you." This morning in bed, from 6:30 am to 7:00 am, K explained to Ro both the creation story in Genesis and the theory of evolution. Ro had asked, "Where do people come from?"

through my nose, my mouth

December 13, 2020

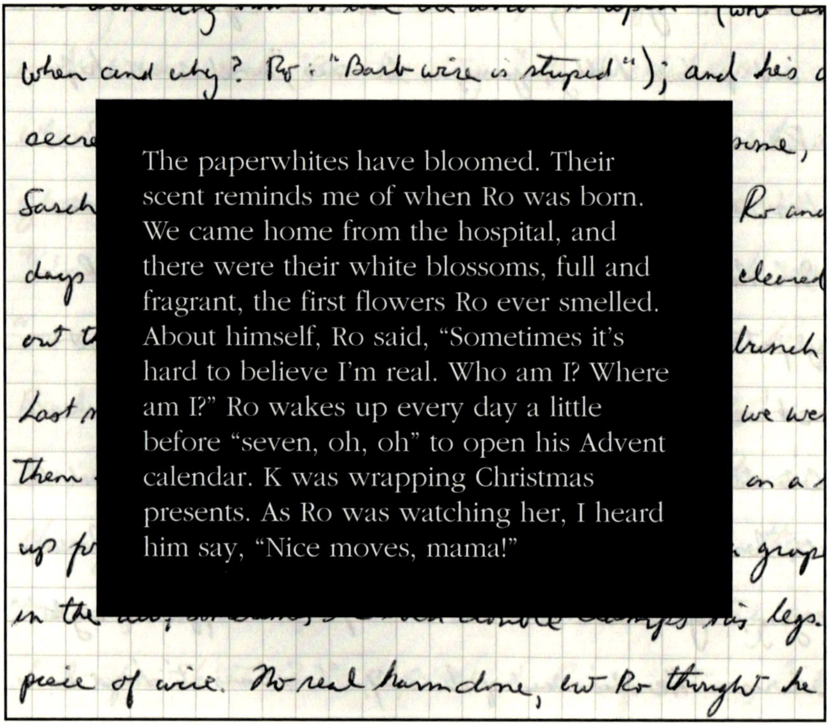

The paperwhites have bloomed. Their scent reminds me of when Ro was born. We came home from the hospital, and there were their white blossoms, full and fragrant, the first flowers Ro ever smelled. About himself, Ro said, "Sometimes it's hard to believe I'm real. Who am I? Where am I?" Ro wakes up every day a little before "seven, oh, oh" to open his Advent calendar. K was wrapping Christmas presents. As Ro was watching her, I heard him say, "Nice moves, mama!"

how the fabric of your mask pulsed

December 20, 2020

K and Ro made sugar cookies using a kit from Fluff Bakery: blank cookies, ready for icing and sprinkles. When they went to pick them up, she and Ro ended up getting their picture in the *Athens News,* sort of. It started snowing, and the *Athens News* posted a shot of "Snow falling on Court Street." And there was our car, on Court Street, pulling into a parking space in front of Fluff. As for the snow, we had a few inches and did some sledding, including Turkey Hill. Ro said it was "epic." He didn't like when snow sprayed up into his face. We also had mini-snowball fights. Ro prefers to be the one who throws the snowballs and for us to be the targets. He and I also built "a snow amusement park." We packed his slide with snow, then extended it with even more snow, so he could have an extralong, face-first slide. After we came in, Ro worried there might be coyotes around. Was our snowman safe? "Snowmen are great," I said, "but they aren't made of meat." In the middle of the night, K awoke with a dripping wet sock on her face. Huh? She felt the bed. Also wet. She felt Ro. Dry. She removed the wet sheet from the bed and found Ro's purple water bottle. He must have woken

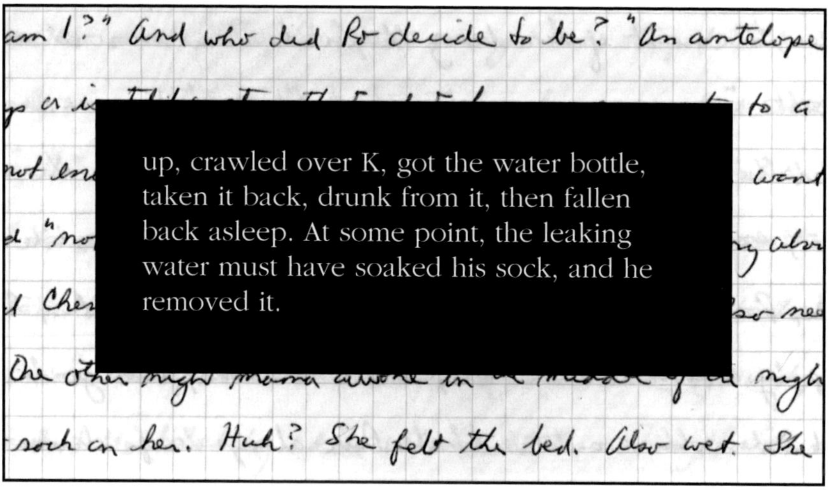

up, crawled over K, got the water bottle, taken it back, drunk from it, then fallen back asleep. At some point, the leaking water must have soaked his sock, and he removed it.

beneath your fear-bright eyes

December 27, 2020

For the winter solstice, we hung solar-powered "fairy lights" in the nearby grove, at the hilltop, and in the far pines. Later that night, we went for a walk in the rain and watched them twinkle. We also ate frozen blackcap berries we'd saved from summer. The next day, I drove to Columbus to meet Gmaw and Gpaw at a public park for a socially distant present swap. Then came Christmas. Ro awoke at 6:57 am. We looked out the window. Seven inches of snow! We immediately opened a few presents. The Transformers are the big hit: Hotshot, Whirl, Wedge, and Hoist. Hoist is a cement truck and Ro's favorite. (Throughout the day, Ro transformed them at least five hundred times. Click, click. Click, click.) For breakfast, we ate cheesy eggs, crumb buns, and babka. We went outside. Ro crawled caterpillar-style in the snow. It was so fluffy we couldn't sled on it or pack it for snowballs, but it was fun to roll in. Ro played "Tackle Mama." After thawing out and drying off, he opened a special present: a red helmet. "Did I get a bike?" Out came the bike. I cleared a circuit around the porch, and Ro tried it out, smiling each time he rode by.

(Later, he asked, “How many dollars is it?”) Inside for ham, rolls, collard greens, scalloped potatoes, mashed potatoes, gravy, and a beet, goat cheese, walnut, and pomegranate salad. K and I finished the meal and resolved never to eat again. Ro was ready for some downtime. We did a few FaceTime calls with family and, afterward, more presents. At bedtime, Ro wore his new buffalo-plaid pj’s and fell asleep fast. The letdown the next day was rough. Also, the washer broke. It won’t drain. I have to take out the waterlogged clothes and wring them in the shower stall, then go back to the washer and scoop out the dirty water with a cup and a bucket. (I’m trying to get K and Ro to change their clothes less often.) Today the snow is melting.

January 4, 2021

Ro and I started 2021 by patching up the ventilation system beneath the house. In the crawlspace. In the cold. In the dark. Here's the context: A few days ago, a repairman came and supposedly fixed our washer. Then, on New Year's Day, the washer flooded the entire kitchen. Water spilled across the floor and into one of the air vents, filling the vent hose that runs underneath it and pulling it down with water weight. Ro loved it. In the crawlspace, he held the flashlight and used his "smallness power" to carry out water and dump it in the yard as the official head of the "Bucket Brigade." Happy New Year! On the third, Ro turned five. He was up at 4:30 am, which made for a long wait. In the final minutes, he started doing a kind of furious Hokey Pokey. On to presents, including a remote-control monster truck and twin guitars, one Ro-sized and one K-sized. Afterward, we took a short walk, and the woods celebrated Ro: A hawk flew over him and made its "Ro!" cry, bluejays followed him, and the pine trees left him a fallen branch with five baby pinecones on it. We also went geocaching. Our first search was by the library. Ro liked being sneaky and making sure the "Muggles"—

those normal people who don't know about the geocache—didn't spot him. We found the cache. From the toys inside it, Ro selected a pink plastic dolphin figurine. The next cache was at the Athens Visitors Center. In the bushes, Ro found a bright orange box and chose from it a silly putty egg. We chased this high and set off to Sells Park, but the cache that was supposed to be in a hollow tree was gone. Then the battery on K's phone died and, with it, the geocaching app. Heartbreak, fueled by too little sleep and a need for food. After lunch, Ro had a carrot cake decorated with balloon macaroons. In the afternoon, I built a fire, and Ro tried out his new stomp rockets. Soon, friends started coming up the driveway for a birthday parade. They honked. They waved signs with "Happy Birthday, Ro!" They stood out of their sunroofs and hollered. More balloons. At 6:35 pm, we had a moment of recognition to mark the time that Ro was born. He ate a cheeseburger and fries for dinner. Getting into his pajamas, he said, "I feel so full of birthday joy."

on a whisper, a sigh, a song before bed.

January 10, 2021

A belated Christmas present arrived for Ro: a bug-catching kit with plastic tongs and a plastic specimen jar. On our morning walk, Ro took it with him. He tonged rocks, grass, and the bark off trees. When we reached a nearby pine, he tonged a little moss off the ground and put the moss in the jar. He tried to get the lid on the jar. He couldn't. He asked me to put the lid on the jar. I did. We restarted our walk, but Ro saw more moss. "I wish I had that moss, too." I breathed. I accepted that we were moving at the pace of a child exploring natural world. "You can get that moss, too," I said. Ro opened the jar and put a second clump of moss in the jar. He tried to get the lid on the jar. He couldn't. "Would you like me to help?" "Yes." I snapped on the lid. Ro took five steps forward, holding the jar sideways. The lid popped off. His moss fell to ground. "Aw!" he said. I breathed. "You can get them again, buddy." We went back to the pine tree. Ro re-tonged both mosses. He tried to put the lid on the jar. He couldn't. I put the lid on the jar. I returned the jar to Ro. He decided to put the jar in his pocket. He couldn't. He shoved it. In it went. We retraced our five steps and reached the grass on other side of driveway. I heard a crack. I felt a crunch under my foot. I looked down at the frozen ground. I saw shards of cheap Chinese plastic. "You stepped on my jar!" This was true. The jar had popped out of Ro's pocket. The jar had landed on ground. The jar had been stepped on. By me. "Yes, but it was an accident, buddy. I wouldn't step on your jar on purpose." I collected the shards of plastic. The shards are sharp, like glass. I put the shards in my pocket. "You broke it," said Ro. "It was my favorite in the whole world." He and I talked about how sad this is, how we will try to find a replacement jar. Ro sighed. He jammed his hands in his pockets and walked away with his head hung down. I tried to engage him. Together, we recounted the story of me breaking his jar. Our sadness. My sorriness. The walk and our spirits improved. Ro skipped ahead, faster and faster. I rushed after him. He suddenly came to a dead stop. I quickly sidestepped, trying not to knock him over. I grazed him. "Papa," he cried, "you stepped on me!" Also this week, a new civil war at the Capitol.

January 17, 2021

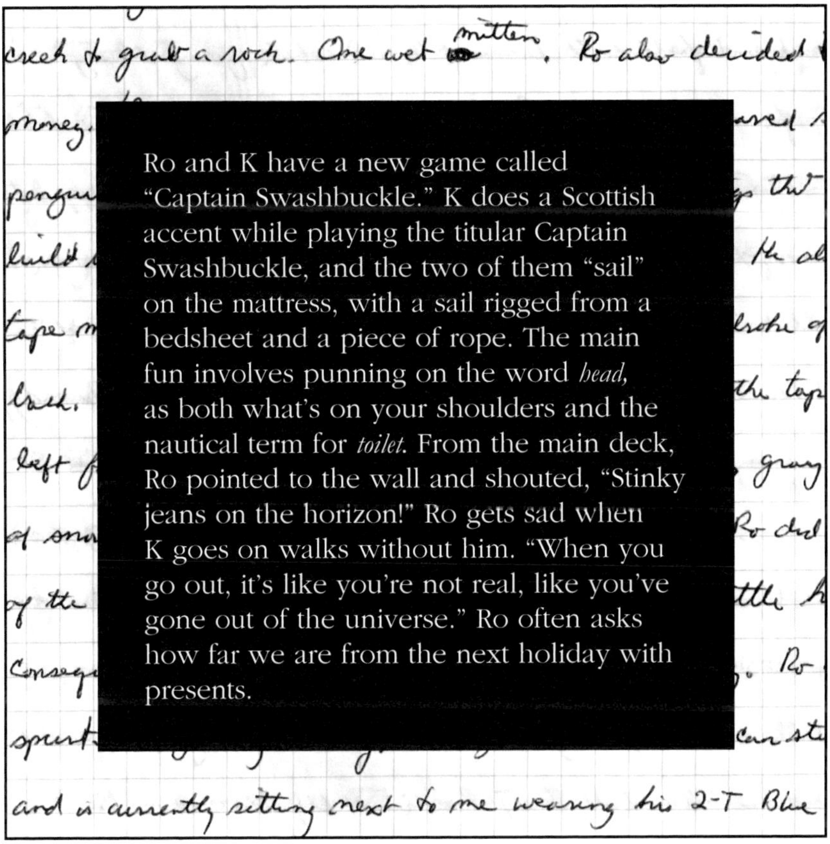

Ro and K have a new game called "Captain Swashbuckle." K does a Scottish accent while playing the titular Captain Swashbuckle, and the two of them "sail" on the mattress, with a sail rigged from a bedsheet and a piece of rope. The main fun involves punning on the word *head,* as both what's on your shoulders and the nautical term for *toilet.* From the main deck, Ro pointed to the wall and shouted, "Stinky jeans on the horizon!" Ro gets sad when K goes on walks without him. "When you go out, it's like you're not real, like you've gone out of the universe." Ro often asks how far we are from the next holiday with presents.

I remember how our house felt

January 24, 2021

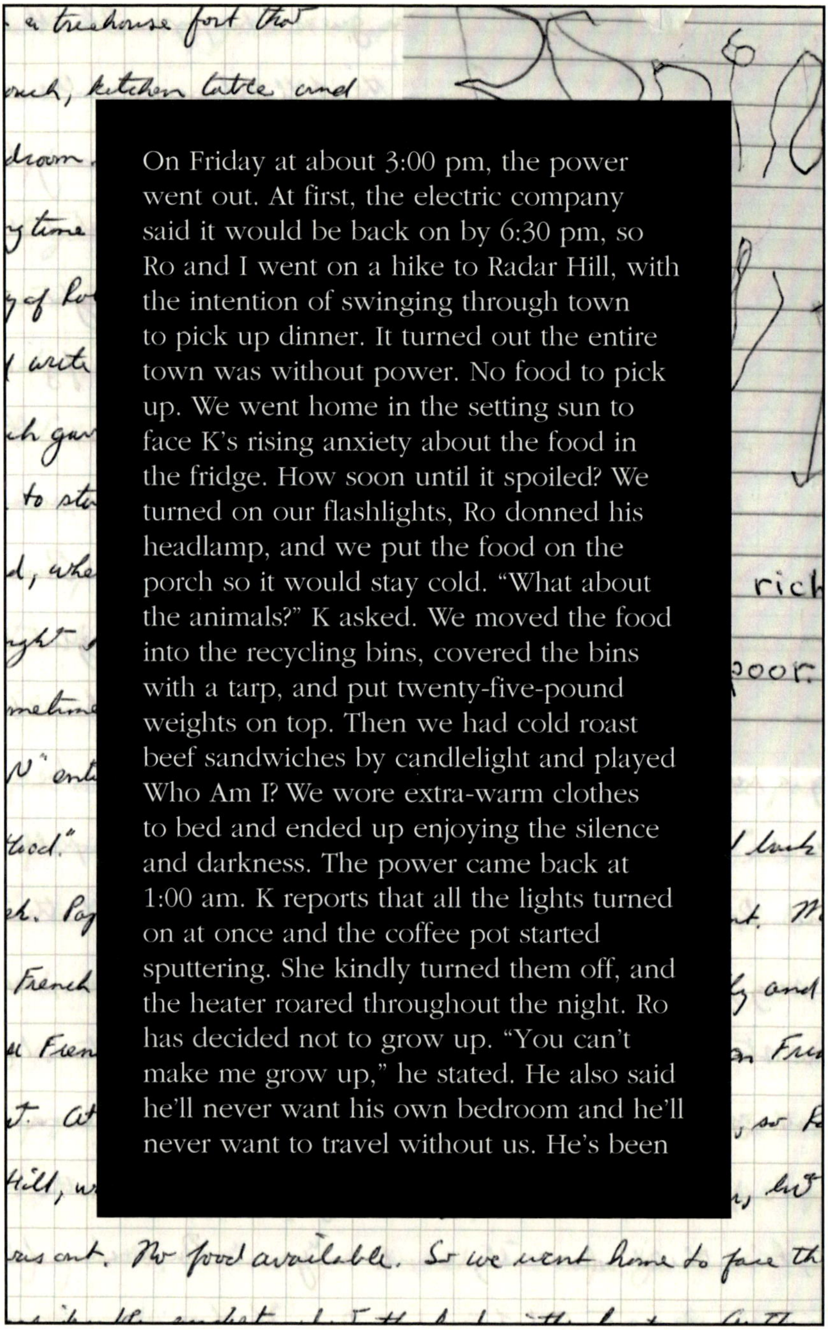

On Friday at about 3:00 pm, the power went out. At first, the electric company said it would be back on by 6:30 pm, so Ro and I went on a hike to Radar Hill, with the intention of swinging through town to pick up dinner. It turned out the entire town was without power. No food to pick up. We went home in the setting sun to face K's rising anxiety about the food in the fridge. How soon until it spoiled? We turned on our flashlights, Ro donned his headlamp, and we put the food on the porch so it would stay cold. "What about the animals?" K asked. We moved the food into the recycling bins, covered the bins with a tarp, and put twenty-five-pound weights on top. Then we had cold roast beef sandwiches by candlelight and played Who Am I? We wore extra-warm clothes to bed and ended up enjoying the silence and darkness. The power came back at 1:00 am. K reports that all the lights turned on at once and the coffee pot started sputtering. She kindly turned them off, and the heater roared throughout the night. Ro has decided not to grow up. "You can't make me grow up," he stated. He also said he'll never want his own bedroom and he'll never want to travel without us. He's been

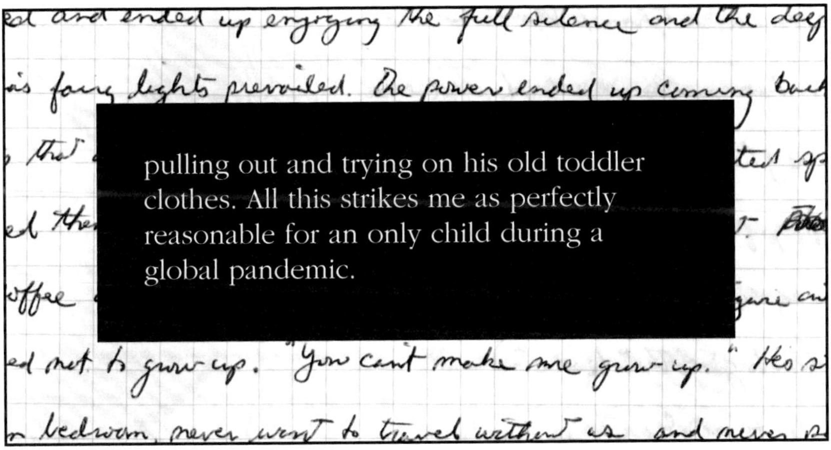

pulling out and trying on his old toddler clothes. All this strikes me as perfectly reasonable for an only child during a global pandemic.

like a lone ship on a green sea.

January 31, 2021

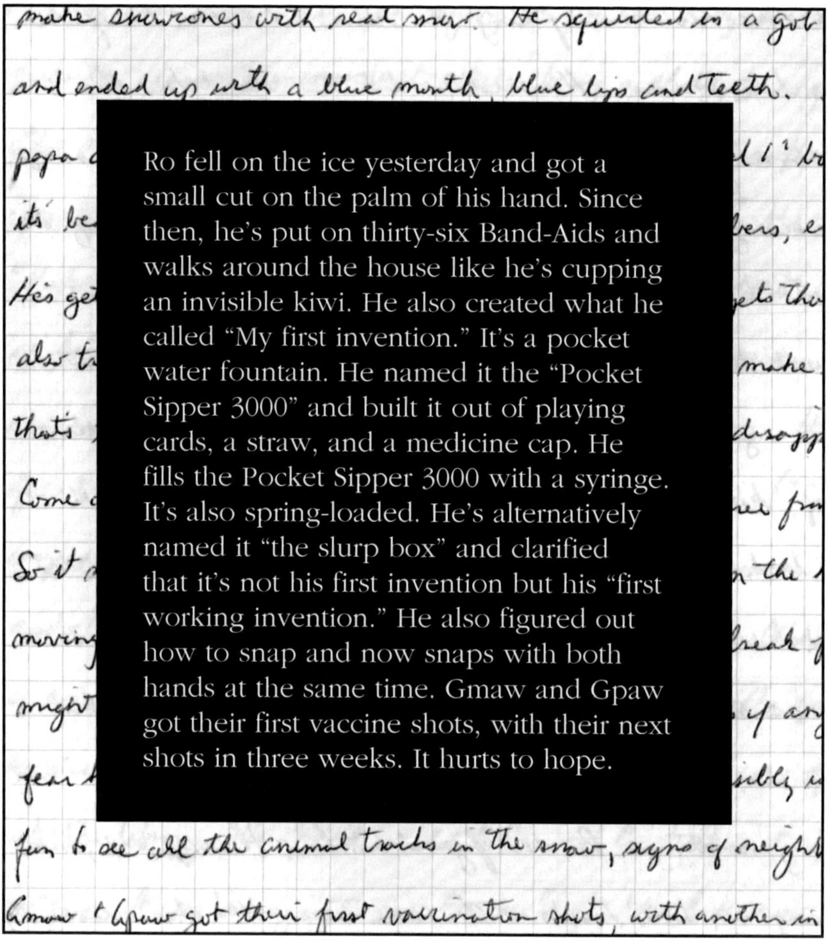

Ro fell on the ice yesterday and got a small cut on the palm of his hand. Since then, he's put on thirty-six Band-Aids and walks around the house like he's cupping an invisible kiwi. He also created what he called "My first invention." It's a pocket water fountain. He named it the "Pocket Sipper 3000" and built it out of playing cards, a straw, and a medicine cap. He fills the Pocket Sipper 3000 with a syringe. It's also spring-loaded. He's alternatively named it "the slurp box" and clarified that it's not his first invention but his "first working invention." He also figured out how to snap and now snaps with both hands at the same time. Gmaw and Gpaw got their first vaccine shots, with their next shots in three weeks. It hurts to hope.

February 7, 2021

From the hilltop to the road, the entire quarter mile of our driveway is a sheet of ice. On Friday, Ro and I were shuffling down to get the mail when we saw the mailman gunning his truck toward the hill. “No!” I yelled and started waving him off. The truck got about halfway up the hill and started spinning, then slid into the ditch and stuck. “Well, here’s your mail,” he said, then added, “The package almost fit in the mailbox.” He asked me to call our neighbor, so he could bring over his tractor and pull out the truck. Once our neighbor arrived, the mailman called his supervisor. Did he want a tow truck? “Think you can do it?” the mailman asked our neighbor. “I know this ain’t your first rodeo.” Our neighbor nodded. (Later, I asked our neighbor how many people he’s pulled from the driveway. “None.”) Our neighbor hooked up a chain to the mail truck’s bumper. The mailman got in. Our neighbor started the tractor and pulled. Immediately, the truck began spinning. Sometimes it looked like the truck was going down the hill, but then it would spin back up. Our neighbor stopped with the mail truck sideways. “Maybe it won’t work!” said Ro. “Maybe we need to call a tow truck!” By now, K had joined us. The two decided to

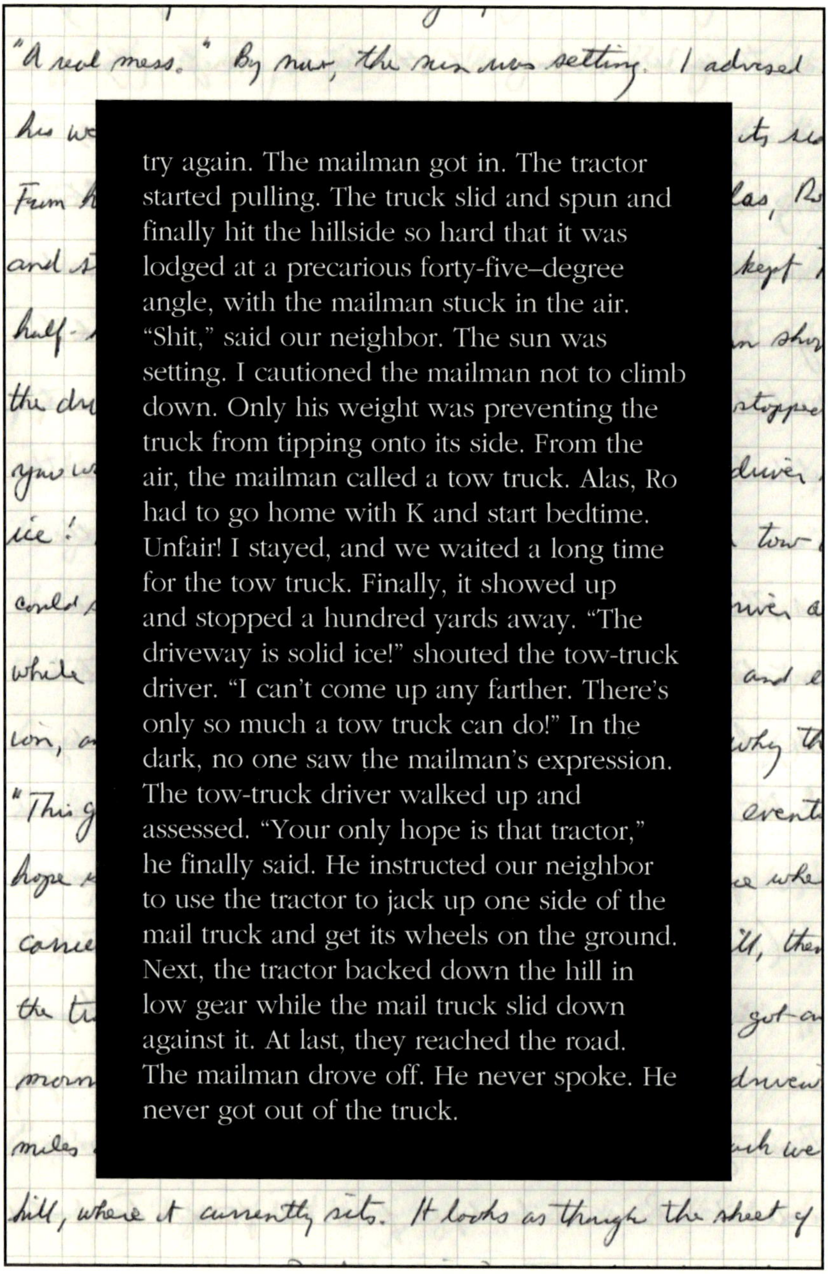
“A real mess.” By now, the sun was setting. I advised

hill, where it currently sits. It looks as though the sheet of

try again. The mailman got in. The tractor started pulling. The truck slid and spun and finally hit the hillside so hard that it was lodged at a precarious forty-five–degree angle, with the mailman stuck in the air. “Shit,” said our neighbor. The sun was setting. I cautioned the mailman not to climb down. Only his weight was preventing the truck from tipping onto its side. From the air, the mailman called a tow truck. Alas, Ro had to go home with K and start bedtime. Unfair! I stayed, and we waited a long time for the tow truck. Finally, it showed up and stopped a hundred yards away. “The driveway is solid ice!” shouted the tow-truck driver. “I can’t come up any farther. There’s only so much a tow truck can do!” In the dark, no one saw the mailman’s expression. The tow-truck driver walked up and assessed. “Your only hope is that tractor,” he finally said. He instructed our neighbor to use the tractor to jack up one side of the mail truck and get its wheels on the ground. Next, the tractor backed down the hill in low gear while the mail truck slid down against it. At last, they reached the road. The mailman drove off. He never spoke. He never got out of the truck.

I remember the numbers that lived online

February 14, 2021

At Fox Lake, near the parking lot, Ro and I found a heap of bloody viscera. It had obviously been dragged into the bushes. (There was a pink streak in the snow.) We also found huge, pink pawprints. I kept Ro away from the guts, and we followed the tracks all around the lake. When we got home, Ro looked them up. Probably a coyote, but at the time, we wondered if it was a bobcat or a bear. The snow and ice have stayed. Another storm is expected tomorrow night. Ro continues enjoying the snow, eating it, sucking on snowballs, and "butt 'bogganing," where he slides down snowy hills on his butt. After he's walked for a little while in the snow, he likes to collapse dramatically, as though into a puffy Victorian fainting couch. Lately, he's been "Frederick the Vampire," saying in a classic vampiric voice, "Gooooood eeeeeeevening!" When I replied, "Gooooood eeeeeeevening!" he said, "That's my line." The costume is crucial. The cape, the teeth. A few days ago, he said, "I've had some hard times in my life as a child." Like what? "Like the time I locked myself in the bathroom, and it took some time for you to get me out." I found an open jar of Vaseline on Ro's desk. "What's this?" I asked. "I was trying to get

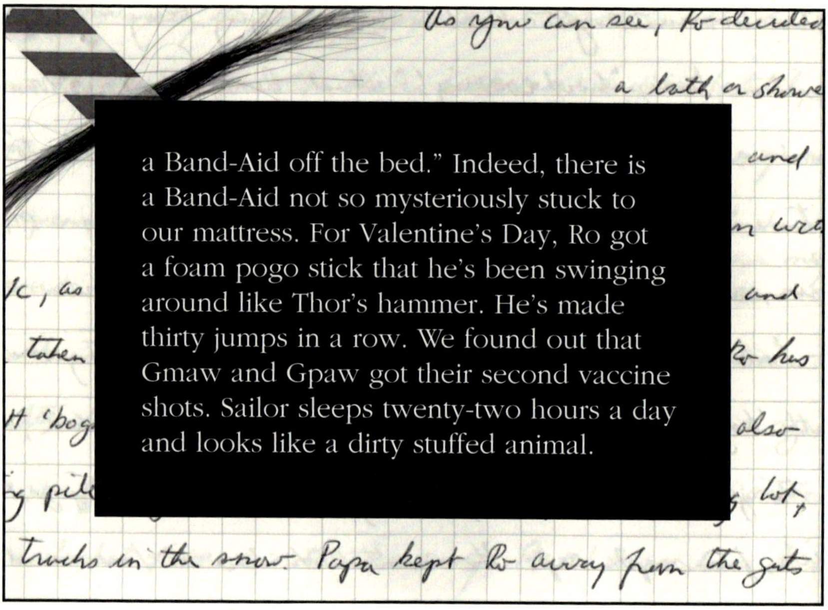

a Band-Aid off the bed." Indeed, there is a Band-Aid not so mysteriously stuck to our mattress. For Valentine's Day, Ro got a foam pogo stick that he's been swinging around like Thor's hammer. He's made thirty jumps in a row. We found out that Gmaw and Gpaw got their second vaccine shots. Sailor sleeps twenty-two hours a day and looks like a dirty stuffed animal.

every day, the infection counts

February 21, 2021

Ro planted an orange seed a few weeks ago, and now the sprout is about six inches high. Today, as he watered it, he poured a splash from a cup, then felt the soil: “Damp, but not wet . . . [adds a little more] Damp, but not wet. . . . [checks soil with his finger] Damp, but not wet . . . ” A cold storm created a sheet of ice over the existing snow, then a few days later it snowed again over the ice. We’ve been parking at the bottom of the driveway and hauling up our groceries in laundry baskets. We also loaded three weeks’ worth of recycling into boxes, put them on a sled, and dragged them down to the road. Earlier today, K took Ro on her knee. “This is how you fool a dog,” she said. She then held out a pretend stick in front of a pretend dog and pretended to throw the pretend stick. “And then, when the dog stops looking for the stick, it turns back to you, and you show him the stick, and the dog goes, ‘What!?’” This morning, Ro woke up at 6:00 am and couldn’t fall back asleep. I heard him softly saying, “One sheep . . . Two sheep . . . Three sheep . . . ”

every day, the death counts.

February 28, 2021

Charlie Chaplin was featured in one of Ro's cartoons and piqued his interest. K showed him a few old film clips. Now he's enthralled. All the more so because we got him a Charlie Chaplin costume: top hat, long coat, vest, boutonniere, and, as Ro said, "Of course, floppy pants!" We also got him a bamboo cane that's curved at the top. (I sawed off the end to shorten it.) For the last few days, Ro-as-Charlie has been waddling around the house, bumping into walls, then taking off his hat, tipping it to the wall, and saying, "I beg your pardon!" He's also made one roller skate so he can recreate the "skating blindfold" scene from *Modern Times.* He's done Charlie for our neighbors and, on screen, for Gmaw and Gpaw. He hates stepping out of character. "It's just so hard to stop being Charlie!" (As I write, he's standing on the couch in his Charlie costume, holding his cane, once again watching the cartoon.) With K, he plays "What Would Charlie Do?" In a given situation, they speculate about what kind of "gags" Charlie might do, then Ro enacts them. He's also come up with his own Charlie gags, including putting confetti in his hat and trying to scooch his sled forward using only his cane, then saying, "It's a fine day for sledding!" At bedtime,

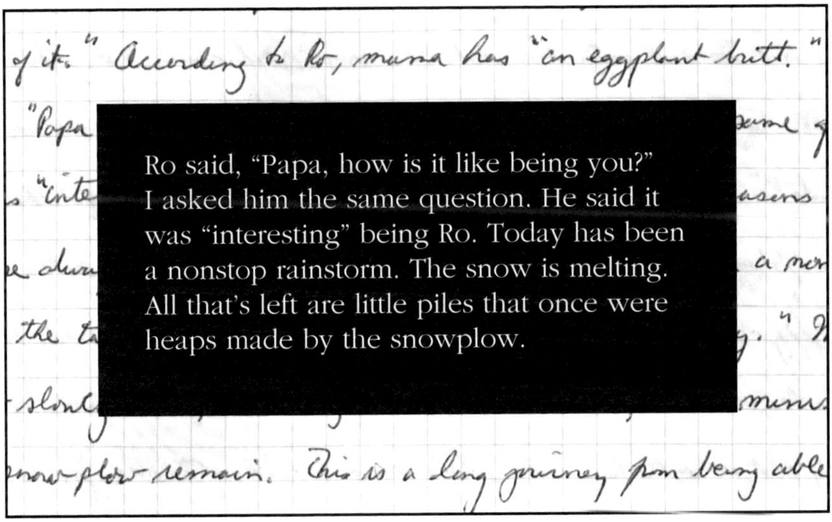

Ro said, "Papa, how is it like being you?" I asked him the same question. He said it was "interesting" being Ro. Today has been a nonstop rainstorm. The snow is melting. All that's left are little piles that once were heaps made by the snowplow.

March 7, 2021

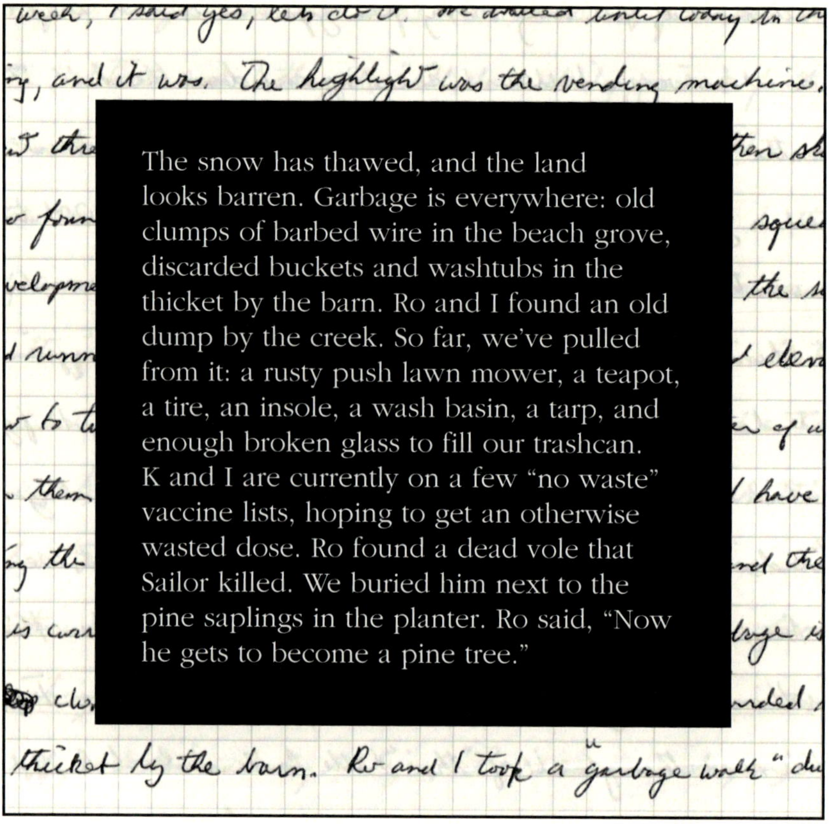

The snow has thawed, and the land looks barren. Garbage is everywhere: old clumps of barbed wire in the beach grove, discarded buckets and washtubs in the thicket by the barn. Ro and I found an old dump by the creek. So far, we've pulled from it: a rusty push lawn mower, a teapot, a tire, an insole, a wash basin, a tarp, and enough broken glass to fill our trashcan. K and I are currently on a few "no waste" vaccine lists, hoping to get an otherwise wasted dose. Ro found a dead vole that Sailor killed. We buried him next to the pine saplings in the planter. Ro said, "Now he gets to become a pine tree."

I remember Amazon rainforests in flames

March 14, 2021

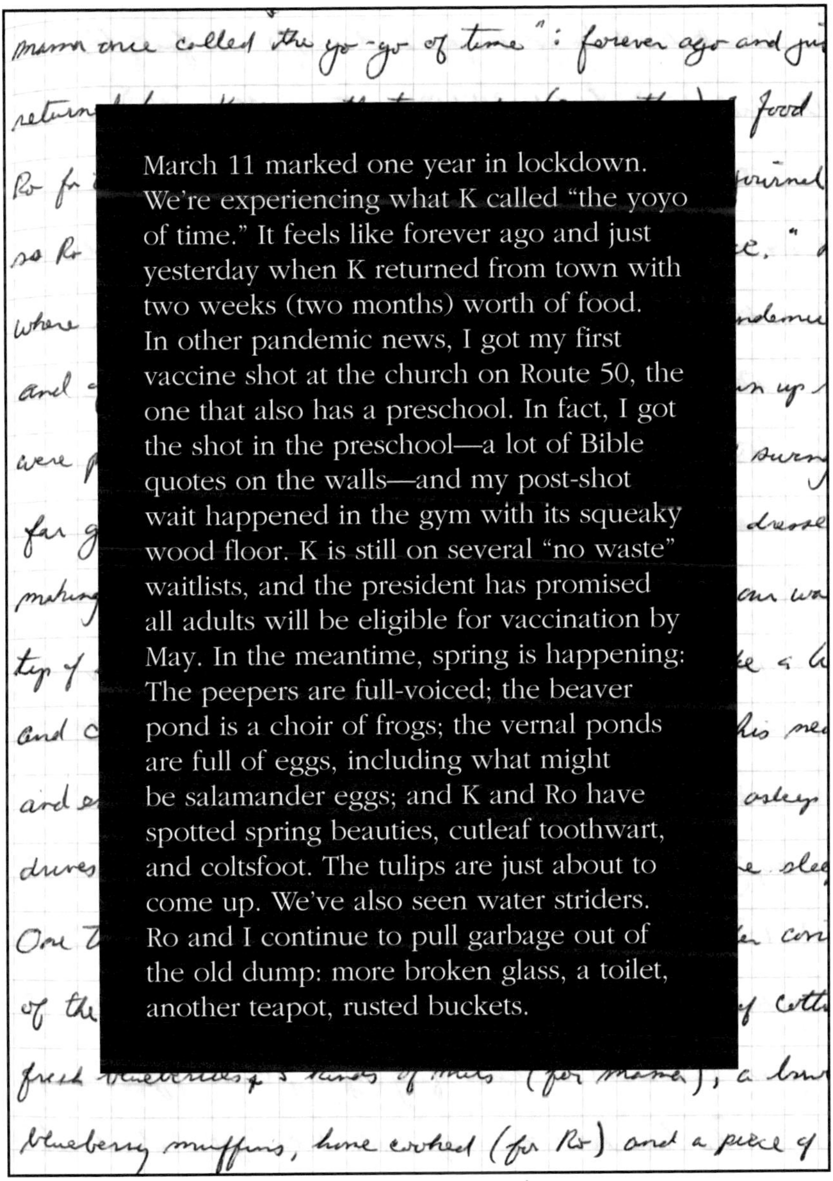

March 11 marked one year in lockdown. We're experiencing what K called "the yoyo of time." It feels like forever ago and just yesterday when K returned from town with two weeks (two months) worth of food. In other pandemic news, I got my first vaccine shot at the church on Route 50, the one that also has a preschool. In fact, I got the shot in the preschool—a lot of Bible quotes on the walls—and my post-shot wait happened in the gym with its squeaky wood floor. K is still on several "no waste" waitlists, and the president has promised all adults will be eligible for vaccination by May. In the meantime, spring is happening: The peepers are full-voiced; the beaver pond is a choir of frogs; the vernal ponds are full of eggs, including what might be salamander eggs; and K and Ro have spotted spring beauties, cutleaf toothwart, and coltsfoot. The tulips are just about to come up. We've also seen water striders. Ro and I continue to pull garbage out of the old dump: more broken glass, a toilet, another teapot, rusted buckets.

entire hillsides of charred trees

March 21, 2021

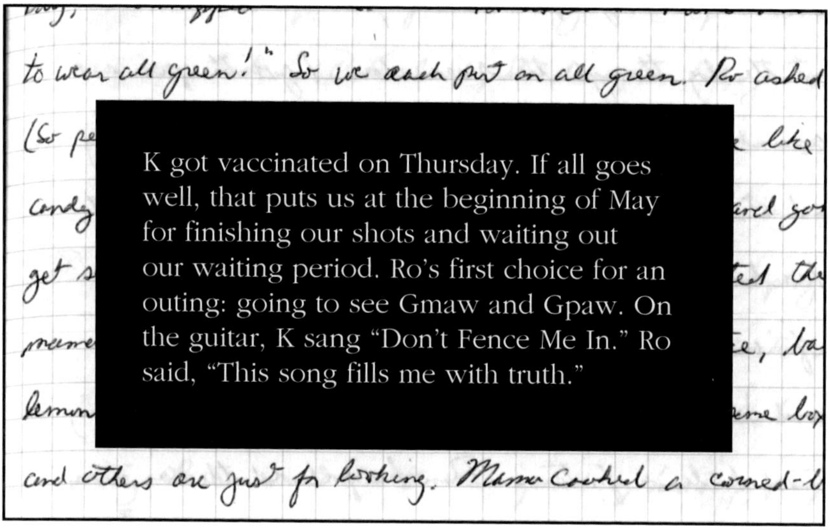

K got vaccinated on Thursday. If all goes well, that puts us at the beginning of May for finishing our shots and waiting out our waiting period. Ro's first choice for an outing: going to see Gmaw and Gpaw. On the guitar, K sang "Don't Fence Me In." Ro said, "This song fills me with truth."

thick white smoke smearing the blank sky.

March 28, 2020

Ro has been tending the sprouts in his window box. He and K planted poppies, nasturtium, kale, lettuce, bachelor's buttons, sunflowers, lemon basil, lemon balm, and chives. Some boxes have nibble-able things, and others are just for looking. Ro got a new pink watering can. As he pours water from the spout, he says, "Drink up." We've been having dance parties. K strums and sings. Ro and I dance. At some point, I always wrap Ro in the rainbow silks from the toybox. I lift him up and spin him through the air the way I used to back when we'd dance at Mini Maestros. I love the serene grin he gets on his face as he spins, eyes half-closed, the silks trailing their crayon colors behind him, red, yellow, blue.

April 4, 2021

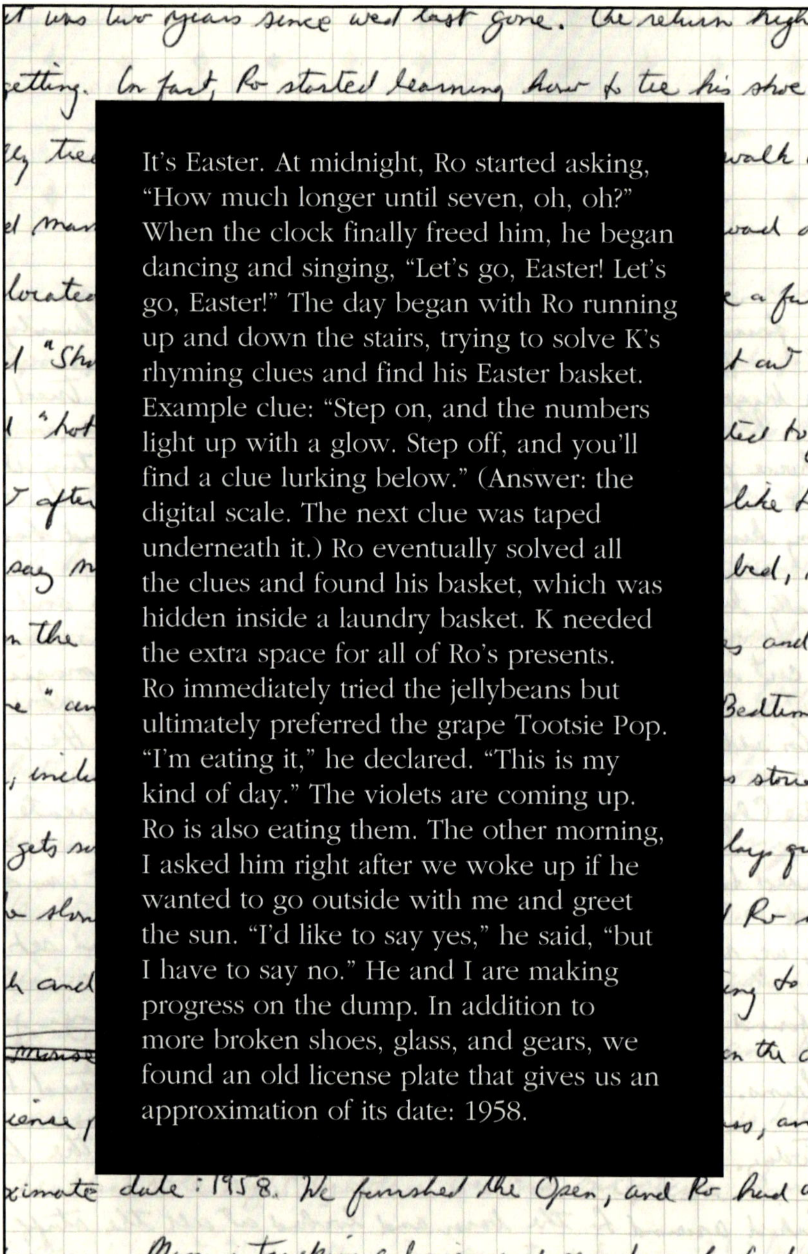

It's Easter. At midnight, Ro started asking, "How much longer until seven, oh, oh?" When the clock finally freed him, he began dancing and singing, "Let's go, Easter! Let's go, Easter!" The day began with Ro running up and down the stairs, trying to solve K's rhyming clues and find his Easter basket. Example clue: "Step on, and the numbers light up with a glow. Step off, and you'll find a clue lurking below." (Answer: the digital scale. The next clue was taped underneath it.) Ro eventually solved all the clues and found his basket, which was hidden inside a laundry basket. K needed the extra space for all of Ro's presents. Ro immediately tried the jellybeans but ultimately preferred the grape Tootsie Pop. "I'm eating it," he declared. "This is my kind of day." The violets are coming up. Ro is also eating them. The other morning, I asked him right after we woke up if he wanted to go outside with me and greet the sun. "I'd like to say yes," he said, "but I have to say no." He and I are making progress on the dump. In addition to more broken shoes, glass, and gears, we found an old license plate that gives us an approximation of its date: 1958.

I remember how I watched you

April 11, 2021

Ro and K made up a call and response. K sings "Hot dog!" Ro sings, "Butt dog!" K: "Snot dog!" Ro: "Butt dog!" K: "Rot dog!" Ro: "Butt dog!" K: "Not dog!" Ro: "Butt dog!" The end. Ro and I just got back from a long walk, where he counted by ones to a thousand. He was very excited, as were the trolls under the bridge when he told them about it. Yesterday, Ro and I visited our old friends D and N, who are now vaccinated. He had a great time in their garden, picking and nibbling various veggies and herbs. When it was time to leave, I asked if Ro if wanted to stay and play with them or go with me to pick up groceries. Easy choice. Off I went, and Ro spent his first time with someone else without K or me nearby. When I got back, he and N were sitting in lawn chairs on the porch, chatting. The thought of D and N moving away is hard, although right now there's no interest in their house, so we'll see. Ro has had difficulty sleeping. Once because of "the Irish song." Which one? "It was just kind of Irish." Once because he woke from a bad dream about a giant creature stomping around. The next morning, he said, "After papa took the dream, I kind of liked it and brought it back, and we played a giant game of goldfish. Guess what? I didn't win. He won."

for invisible wounds.

April 18, 2021

Ro and I went to put out the garbage and saw that our garbage can had been stolen. I texted our neighbor to ask if we could use his. "Of course you can!" We reported the crime to K. "You've got to be kidding me?!" she said. Then began The Ordeal of the Garbage Can. Do we buy another can, only to have it stolen again? Do we store the garbage can at our house, only to smell its stink? What about raccoons? And what kind of garbage can should we get and where should we get it? Finally, we acted. I dropped off Ro and K at the library playground and went to Lowe's. It was the first time I'd been inside a store in over a year. Very unnerving. I bought a metal can and a set of bungee cords to secure the lid. Our plan is to store the can in the barn and take it down on garbage mornings before the garbage truck comes. Ro used the leftover bungee cords to make a zip line in the backseat of the car. He and K have done some rhyming. "Step on a crack, give your mom a snack!" said K. "Step on a crack, give your kid a snack!" said Ro. He then added, "Mine has more *C*s." He pointed out the *C* sound not only in *kid* but also at the end of *snack*. In the mornings, in the nearby brush, the wild turkeys gobble.

April 25, 2021

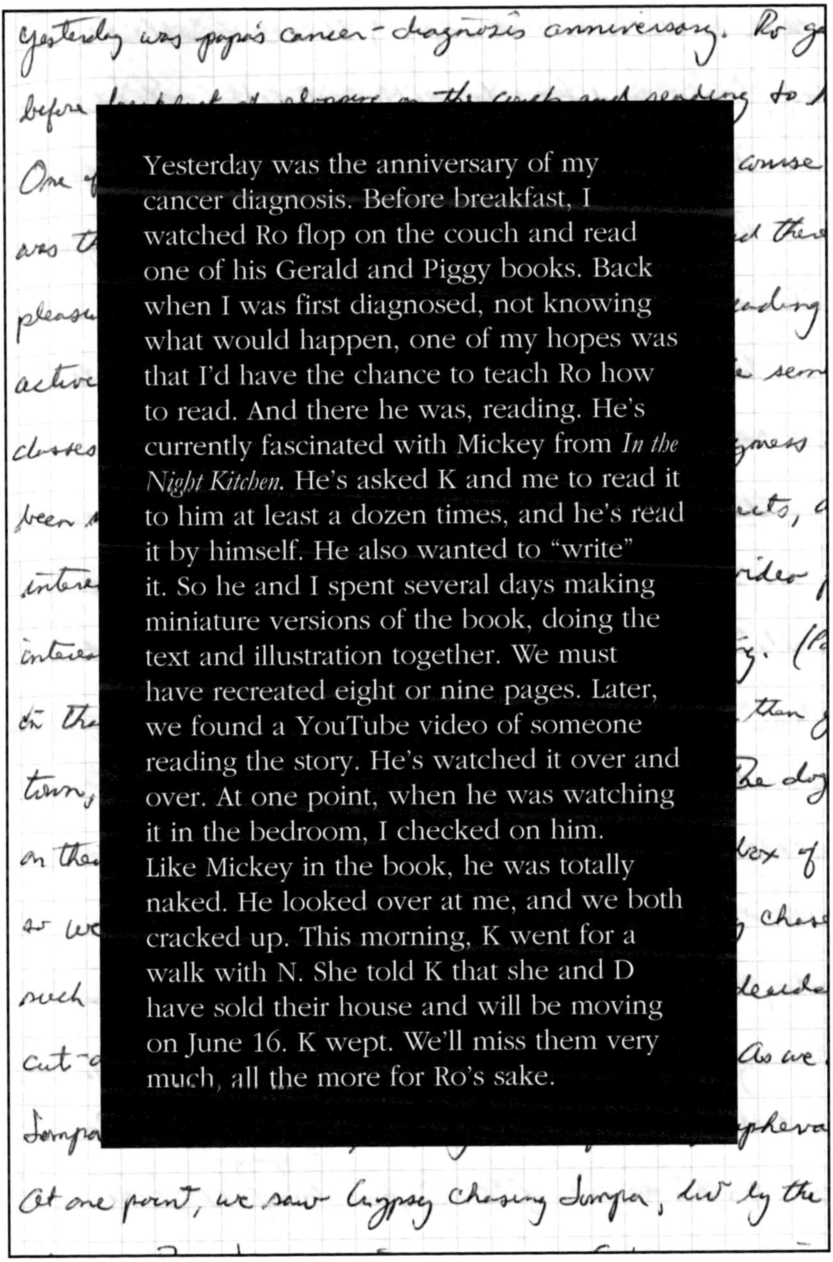

Yesterday was the anniversary of my cancer diagnosis. Before breakfast, I watched Ro flop on the couch and read one of his Gerald and Piggy books. Back when I was first diagnosed, not knowing what would happen, one of my hopes was that I'd have the chance to teach Ro how to read. And there he was, reading. He's currently fascinated with Mickey from *In the Night Kitchen*. He's asked K and me to read it to him at least a dozen times, and he's read it by himself. He also wanted to "write" it. So he and I spent several days making miniature versions of the book, doing the text and illustration together. We must have recreated eight or nine pages. Later, we found a YouTube video of someone reading the story. He's watched it over and over. At one point, when he was watching it in the bedroom, I checked on him. Like Mickey in the book, he was totally naked. He looked over at me, and we both cracked up. This morning, K went for a walk with N. She told K that she and D have sold their house and will be moving on June 16. K wept. We'll miss them very much, all the more for Ro's sake.

May 3, 2021

We took our first overnight trip since March 11, 2020. Where did we go? To see Gmaw and Gpaw. For weeks, Ro has wanted to "start preparating." Every day, he'd wake up and ask, "How many days more?" And then, on Saturday, "I can't believe today is Go Day! I can feel it in my guts." When we arrived, we all hugged and cheered. Ro had lots of cuddles with Gmaw and Gpaw, and we all had ice cream sundaes. Afterward, we went for a long walk. On the way back, Gmaw and Ro were holding hands when Gmaw suddenly collapsed. Gpaw and I helped her up and helped her home. Apparently, this has happened four times in the last year. Ro found it scary. Fortunately, Gmaw soon felt better, and we all played on the back porch with a giant bubble wand. Ro changed into his red shirt and blue jeans so he'd match Gpaw. (Ro packed his own suitcase and brought all of his clothes, except socks. No socks.) The next day, we had a gigantic breakfast of eggs, bacon, bread, scones, pepperoni rolls, strawberries, watermelon, and cookies. Then we went to a local park and, at Gmaw's suggestion, fed the ducks and geese. K pelted several goslings in the face with old bread. I saw a giant sign by the pond: "Do not feed the ducks and geese."

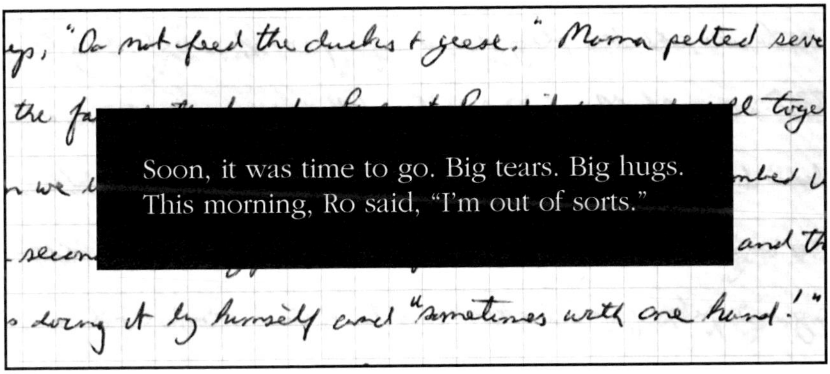

Soon, it was time to go. Big tears. Big hugs. This morning, Ro said, "I'm out of sorts."

on the front page of *The New York Times*

May 9, 2021

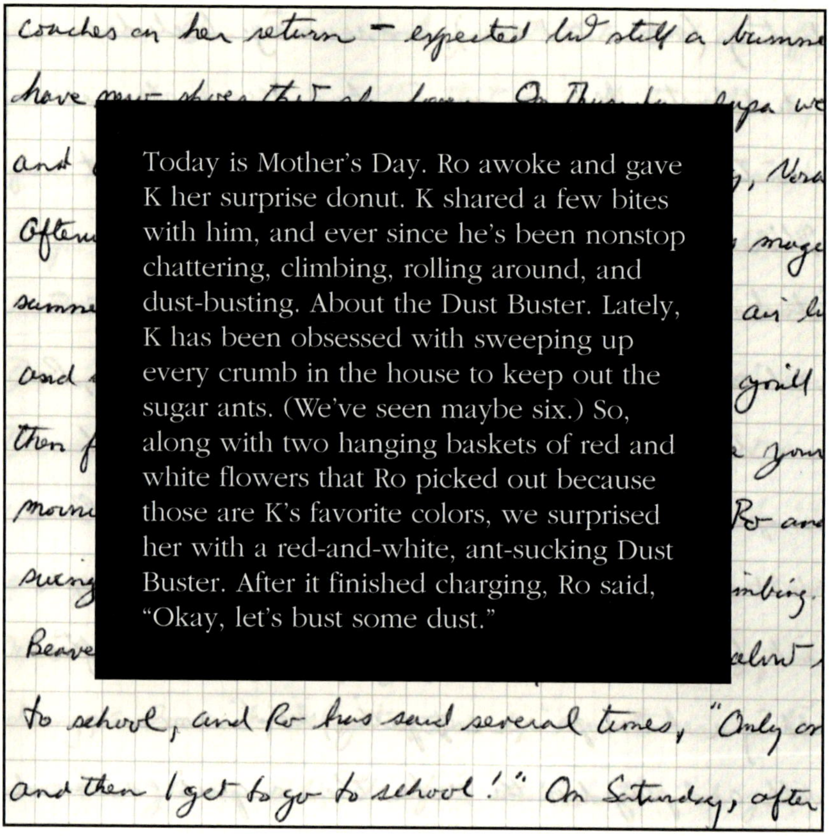

Today is Mother's Day. Ro awoke and gave K her surprise donut. K shared a few bites with him, and ever since he's been nonstop chattering, climbing, rolling around, and dust-busting. About the Dust Buster. Lately, K has been obsessed with sweeping up every crumb in the house to keep out the sugar ants. (We've seen maybe six.) So, along with two hanging baskets of red and white flowers that Ro picked out because those are K's favorite colors, we surprised her with a red-and-white, ant-sucking Dust Buster. After it finished charging, Ro said, "Okay, let's bust some dust."

They were not simply names on a list, it said

May 16, 2021

Ro has a surprise playdate at the farm where he'll hopefully go to school one day. How? For weeks, K had been planning to have dinner with some mothers from the school. At the last moment, Ro and I heard from one of the fathers. Did we want to join them at the farm for pizza and a fire? I asked Ro. "I'm going to play with other kids!" he shouted. On the way through town, we picked up the pizza and some beer. When we arrived, Ro joined the other kids: climbing fences, searching for four-leaf clovers, eating wild sorrel, climbing a giant pile of mulch. (Later, he told me, "I felt shy at first.") Then one of the kids who is currently in the school said, "Can we go to Brambly Hedge?" Suddenly, I was chasing after seven kids who were running at full speed to some spot on the farm named after a children's book about mice living peacefully in the English countryside. Ro took the lead, and a kid shouted, "Ro, you don't know where it is!" A quarter of a mile later, we arrived at Brambly Hedge: a semi-cleared patch of woods cut out of vines, autumn olive, and other brush. The kids from the school took their places in their personal "dens." Ro got his very own den, which he shared with me. He decided his name in Brambly Hedge would be

"Fitz." The kids also took turns on a nearby swinging rope. Most wore "protection suits" as they swung over the crocodile-infested lava pit beneath the rope, but Ro decided to forego the suit and be "daring." When the sun set, we had a fire. A few kids started melting down. (Ro asked, "What's melting down?") We said our goodbyes and went to pick up K. As we drove home in the dark, Ro felt enticed by the idea of falling asleep in the car. He didn't, but he did wake up at 8:00 am this morning, looking tired.

May 24, 2021

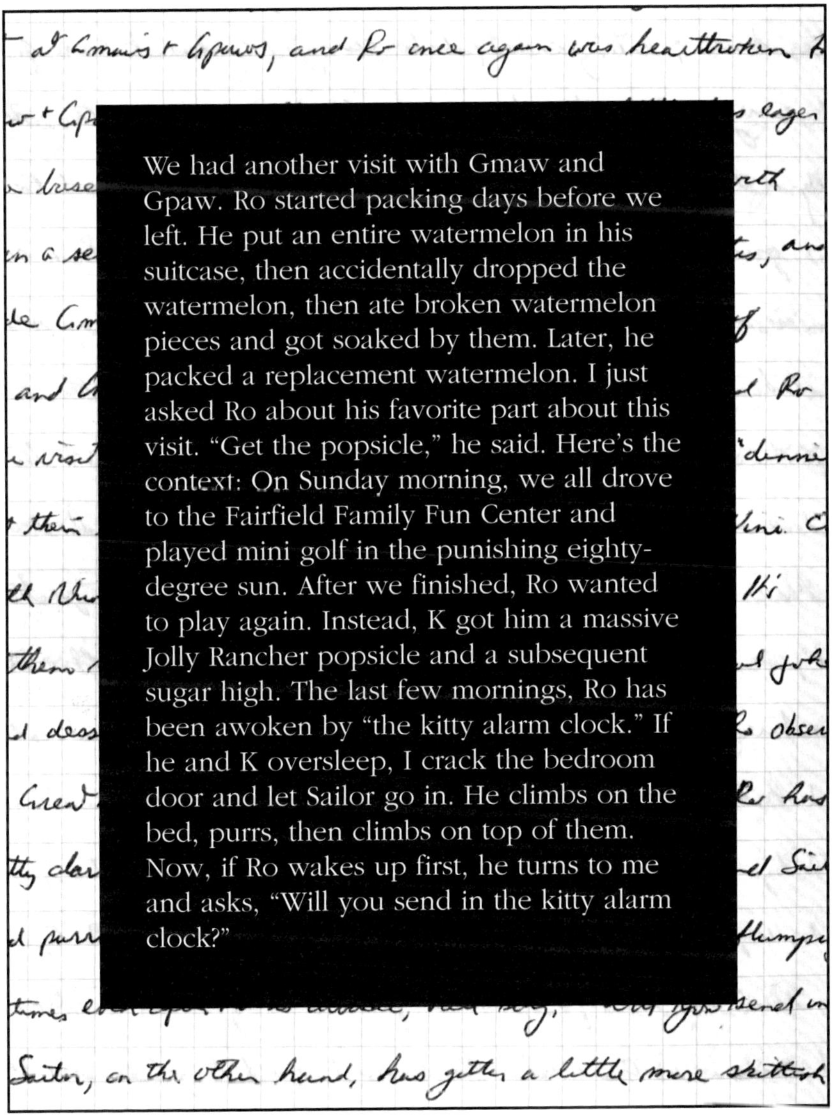

We had another visit with Gmaw and Gpaw. Ro started packing days before we left. He put an entire watermelon in his suitcase, then accidentally dropped the watermelon, then ate broken watermelon pieces and got soaked by them. Later, he packed a replacement watermelon. I just asked Ro about his favorite part about this visit. "Get the popsicle," he said. Here's the context: On Sunday morning, we all drove to the Fairfield Family Fun Center and played mini golf in the punishing eighty-degree sun. After we finished, Ro wanted to play again. Instead, K got him a massive Jolly Rancher popsicle and a subsequent sugar high. The last few mornings, Ro has been awoken by "the kitty alarm clock." If he and K oversleep, I crack the bedroom door and let Sailor go in. He climbs on the bed, purrs, then climbs on top of them. Now, if Ro wakes up first, he turns to me and asks, "Will you send in the kitty alarm clock?"

May 30, 2021

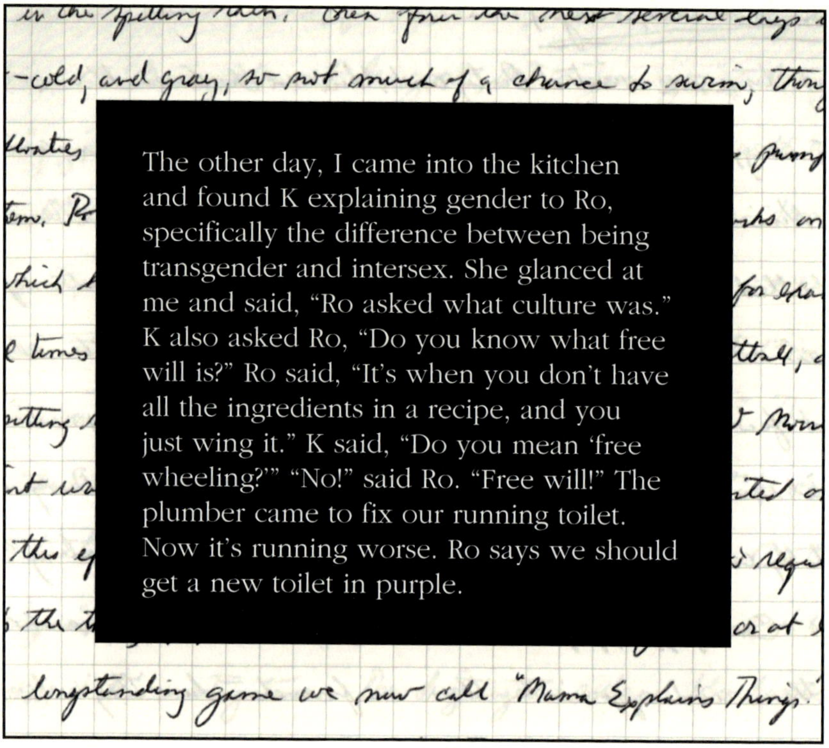

The other day, I came into the kitchen and found K explaining gender to Ro, specifically the difference between being transgender and intersex. She glanced at me and said, "Ro asked what culture was." K also asked Ro, "Do you know what free will is?" Ro said, "It's when you don't have all the ingredients in a recipe, and you just wing it." K said, "Do you mean 'free wheeling?'" "No!" said Ro. "Free will!" The plumber came to fix our running toilet. Now it's running worse. Ro says we should get a new toilet in purple.

I remember how we read the same storybooks

June 6, 2021

We visited D and N for the last time. (As I write, they're on their way to Philadelphia.) When we got to their house, Ro grabbed N, and off they went, sneaking and exploring. K and I chatted with D about the upcoming move and the last-minute repairs. K wanted to know what meals they'd eat on the road. We all played hide-and-seek. D hid on the toilet, which delighted Ro. Over pizza, I told D and N how much we love them, how they welcomed us and were there for Ro's birth, my cancer surgeries, and Ro growing up. Before we left, N gave Ro "his" special cat cup, as well as a strawberry lip balm that scented our drive home. The other day, as we were eating lunch on the porch, a doe came out of the woods, checked us out, walked away, circled back more closely, checked us out again, then disappeared into the woods in exactly the same spot where she had emerged. Sailor watched, frozen, from the high grass.

June 14, 2021

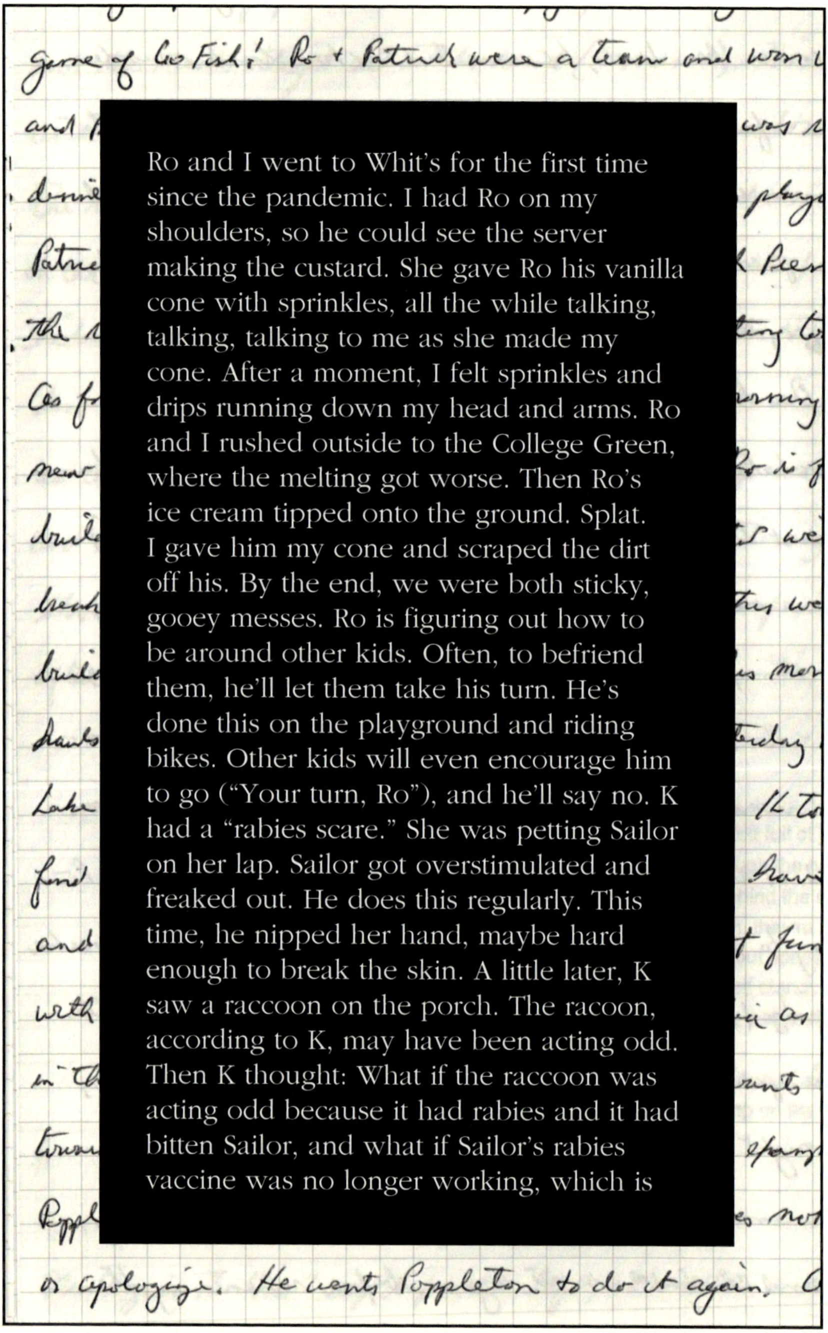
Game of Go Fish! Ro + Patrick were a team and won

or apologize. He wants Poppleton to do it again.

Ro and I went to Whit's for the first time since the pandemic. I had Ro on my shoulders, so he could see the server making the custard. She gave Ro his vanilla cone with sprinkles, all the while talking, talking, talking to me as she made my cone. After a moment, I felt sprinkles and drips running down my head and arms. Ro and I rushed outside to the College Green, where the melting got worse. Then Ro's ice cream tipped onto the ground. Splat. I gave him my cone and scraped the dirt off his. By the end, we were both sticky, gooey messes. Ro is figuring out how to be around other kids. Often, to befriend them, he'll let them take his turn. He's done this on the playground and riding bikes. Other kids will even encourage him to go ("Your turn, Ro"), and he'll say no. K had a "rabies scare." She was petting Sailor on her lap. Sailor got overstimulated and freaked out. He does this regularly. This time, he nipped her hand, maybe hard enough to break the skin. A little later, K saw a raccoon on the porch. The racoon, according to K, may have been acting odd. Then K thought: What if the raccoon was acting odd because it had rabies and it had bitten Sailor, and what if Sailor's rabies vaccine was no longer working, which is

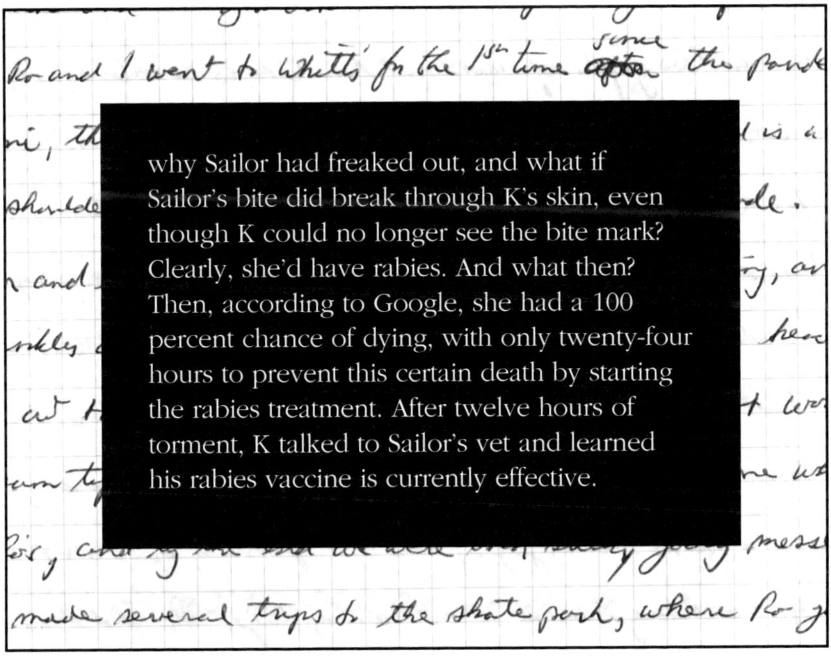

why Sailor had freaked out, and what if Sailor's bite did break through K's skin, even though K could no longer see the bite mark? Clearly, she'd have rabies. And what then? Then, according to Google, she had a 100 percent chance of dying, with only twenty-four hours to prevent this certain death by starting the rabies treatment. After twelve hours of torment, K talked to Sailor's vet and learned his rabies vaccine is currently effective.

a pig decides to buy a bike then buys a bike

June 20, 2021

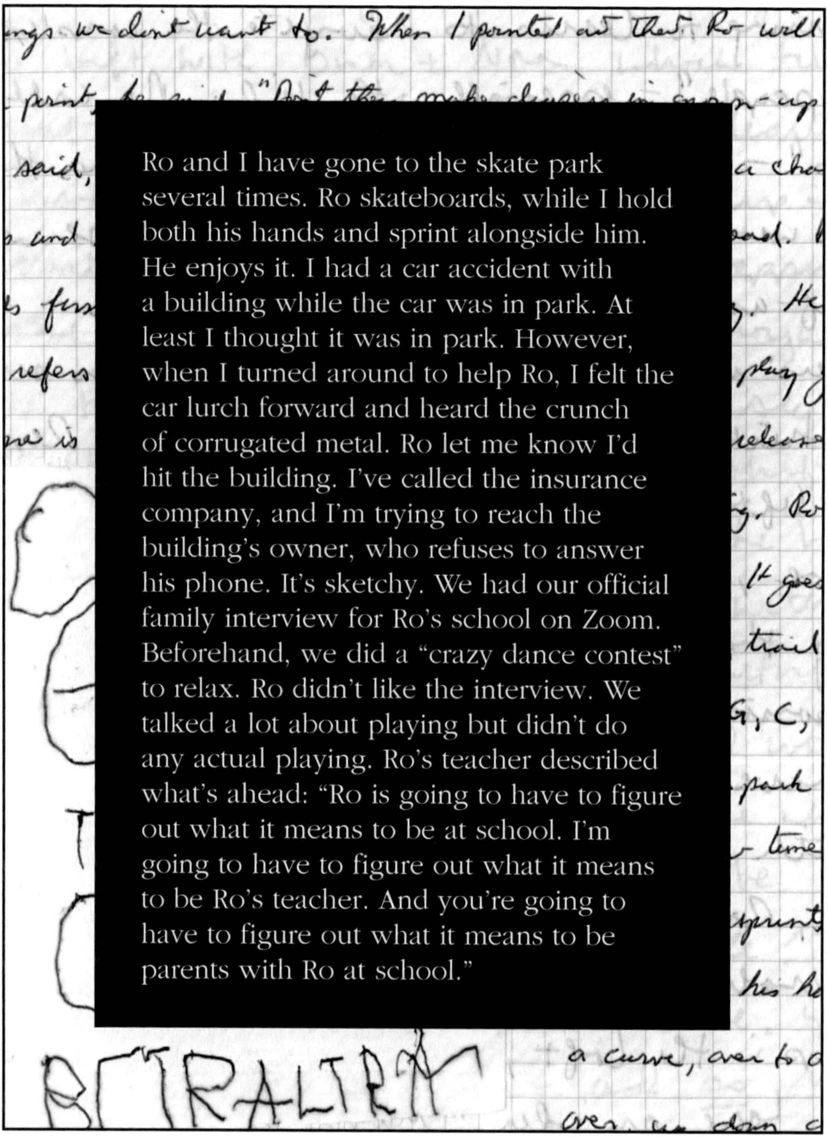

Ro and I have gone to the skate park several times. Ro skateboards, while I hold both his hands and sprint alongside him. He enjoys it. I had a car accident with a building while the car was in park. At least I thought it was in park. However, when I turned around to help Ro, I felt the car lurch forward and heard the crunch of corrugated metal. Ro let me know I'd hit the building. I've called the insurance company, and I'm trying to reach the building's owner, who refuses to answer his phone. It's sketchy. We had our official family interview for Ro's school on Zoom. Beforehand, we did a "crazy dance contest" to relax. Ro didn't like the interview. We talked a lot about playing but didn't do any actual playing. Ro's teacher described what's ahead: "Ro is going to have to figure out what it means to be at school. I'm going to have to figure out what it means to be Ro's teacher. And you're going to have to figure out what it means to be parents with Ro at school."

an old man sits by a window with his cat

June 27, 2021

Ro's favorite bedtime story currently stars Uncle D. It begins with Uncle D filling a trashcan full of Slushie, mixing twenty different flavors, and guzzling it. Uncle D then rides a roller coaster and barfs violently (and, pointedly, not on Ro). After barfing, Uncle D says, "Now we can eat again!" Then Uncle D eats corndogs. Ro likes to direct his bedtime stories. He also likes playing the character that is himself. On Sunday, we celebrated the summer solstice by taking the snow that we'd saved from the freezer and using it for a snowball fight. We also picked some summer berries and froze them for next winter's solstice. Every morning, Ro wakes up and asks, "What's today?"

as snowflakes fall and fall.

July 4, 2021

Yesterday we celebrated Ro's fifth-and-a-half birthday with our friend P. When we arrived at P's house, he had the place decorated with balloons, party hats, and "Happy Birthday" napkins. We bopped balloons. P and Ro built a rocket from Lego. They also played their ritual game of "golf," which involves P bowling a golf ball down the middle of the street toward Ro, who takes a plastic toy golf club and tries to whack the ball as far as possible. K and I chase the ball, usually picking it out of the neighbor's shrubs, while P and Ro laugh. That's the whole game, punctuated by Ro reminding P to take sips of his beer. This time, Ro innovated by hitting the golf ball with a flyswatter. Today, Ro decorated for our Fourth of July party. He strung ribbons and cut out stars to hang on the porch railing. He also designed a sign that says, "Happy!" Our party consisted of just one other family, but we had ample family fun: sack races, three-legged races, egg-on-a-spoon races, tug-of-war, popsicles, and pizza. We set off smoke bombs. Ro chased fireflies for the first time. Even K, after a lifetime of fake-catching fireflies because she never really wanted to catch one because ick, bugs, caught one. We also had a huge rainstorm. Ro hoped we'd lose power.

July 11, 2021

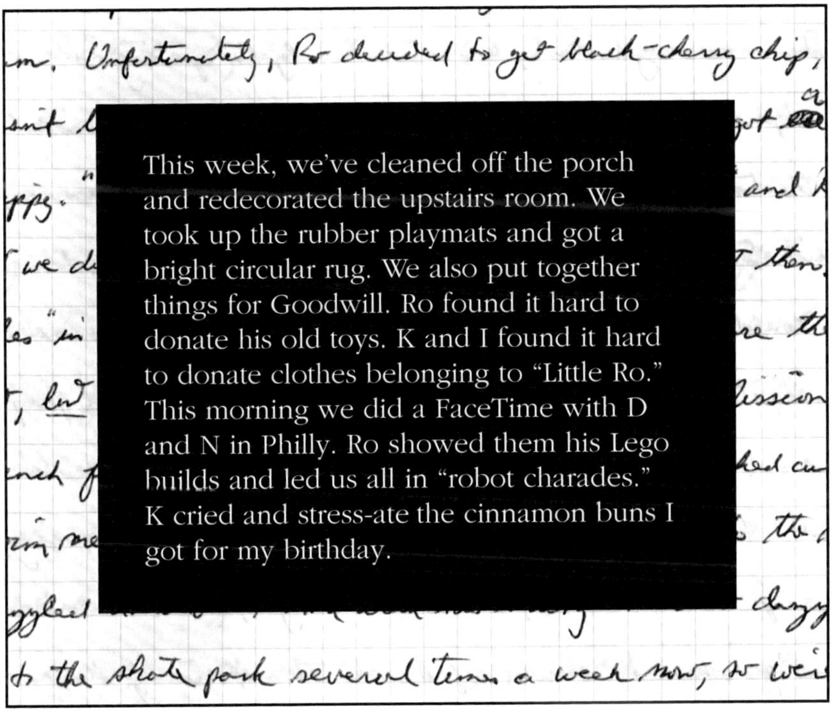

This week, we've cleaned off the porch and redecorated the upstairs room. We took up the rubber playmats and got a bright circular rug. We also put together things for Goodwill. Ro found it hard to donate his old toys. K and I found it hard to donate clothes belonging to "Little Ro." This morning we did a FaceTime with D and N in Philly. Ro showed them his Lego builds and led us all in "robot charades." K cried and stress-ate the cinnamon buns I got for my birthday.

I remember imagining a future

July 18, 2021

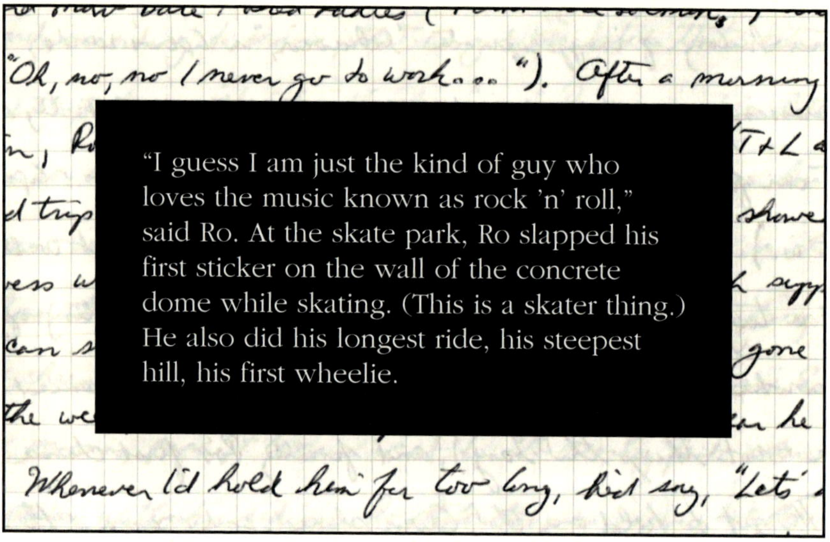

"I guess I am just the kind of guy who loves the music known as rock 'n' roll," said Ro. At the skate park, Ro slapped his first sticker on the wall of the concrete dome while skating. (This is a skater thing.) He also did his longest ride, his steepest hill, his first wheelie.

I might not see.

July 25, 2021

Ro had his first checkup with his new pediatrician. He did well while he was getting weighed and measured, but once the nurse started taking his vitals, he was done. Curiously, when the time came for him to get his booster shots—the only overtly painful part of the visit—he was fine. When it was over, the nurse asked us if it was okay to give Ro "a colored stick." Ro immediately figured out she meant sucker. Grape, please. The next night, he couldn't fall asleep. He said his butt felt "queasy." K reminded me that one of his friends had gotten pinworm. I looked up the symptoms. Yep. We've now all had full doses of pinworm medicine, a vile banana sludge. Ro also has his first loose tooth! He's excited about the Tooth Fairy and let us know he knows the Tooth Fairy is us. K hit a squirrel when we were in the car. I said the squirrel would be a good lunch for a crow. Ro said, "Now it can fly." Later, K was explaining that some people don't understand that trees have feelings and "think they're things like rocks." Ro said, "But rocks have feelings!" Ro also said he couldn't fall asleep because the floor looks like a canyon. What? "I canyon explain it better than that." Over the weekend, Ro had a playdate back at the farm. At the end of it, he said, "I don't want to leave. I want to stay here forever. Can we camp?" He also said goodbye to his friends by offering to shake their hands and saying, "Thank you for playing." At Kroger, I bumped into a pre-pandemic acquaintance. She was with her son, who's Ro's age, and she said her son had just started school. "How is that?" I asked. "It's hard," she said, "just handing over your child that you pour your whole life into." That did sound hard. I feel so grateful we aren't just handing over Ro. We know his school, his teachers, and kids in his class. Even so, we're preparing him for it, putting together his gear and chatting with him about the school's daily schedule and all the things he'll do. As a toddler, Ro used to say, "Yessir-reebee" for "yes." When Ro recalled this, he added, "Did I also say 'no–sir-reebee'?"

August 1, 2021

The Washington Post obtained a PowerPoint that the CDC has presented to Congress: “The war has changed.” There’s now a Delta variant of COVID. It’s more contagious, more dangerous, and vaccinated people can get it and spread it to unvaccinated and vaccinated people alike. I was up until 3:30 am reading about it, staring at case maps that are turning red as the variant spreads from the south toward Athens. K and I did our best to process all the information and concluded that we’re basically back where we were before we were vaccinated: in lockdown. No visits, no playdates, probably no school for Ro. When we told him, he cried. And K cried. I should cry, too, but I’m in survival mode. Ro said, “I feel like a beautiful teacup that broke on a wooden floor into one million, zillion pieces.”

I remember *I can’t breathe*

August 8, 2021

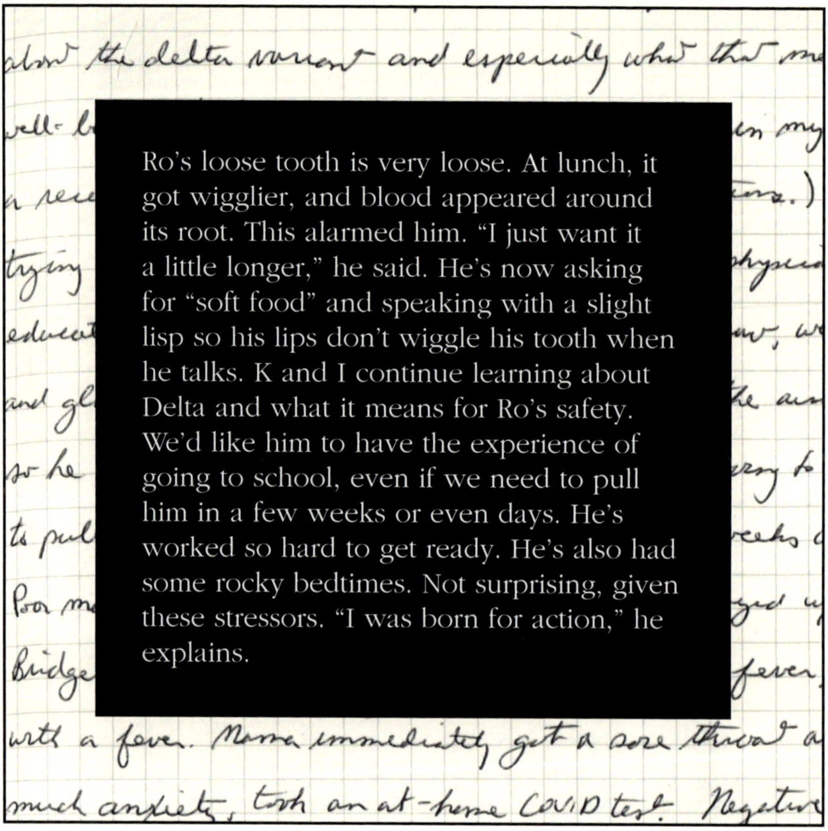

Ro's loose tooth is very loose. At lunch, it got wigglier, and blood appeared around its root. This alarmed him. "I just want it a little longer," he said. He's now asking for "soft food" and speaking with a slight lisp so his lips don't wiggle his tooth when he talks. K and I continue learning about Delta and what it means for Ro's safety. We'd like him to have the experience of going to school, even if we need to pull him in a few weeks or even days. He's worked so hard to get ready. He's also had some rocky bedtimes. Not surprising, given these stressors. "I was born for action," he explains.

as the police murdered George Floyd

August 15, 2021

Ro and I left the house early and drove by the Athens County Fair. It's ominously crowded. Ro expressed sadness "in his heart" at not being able to go. "Will we ever go again?" he asked. I said I didn't know. (I don't.) As we came up West Union, we saw an excavator smashing a big empty building, so we pulled into the parking lot to watch. After a few minutes, Ro said, "You know what would make this even better? A donut." Why not? Before we went on our donut run, I brought up Grubhub and ordered a surprise delivery for D in Philly. It was his birthday, and the best option turned out to be a dizzyingly expensive flight of gourmet smoothies. Then Ro and I drove to McHappy's. Ro got a cake donut with icing and sprinkles, and we circled back to the destruction. Ro liked how the workers used a fire hose to dampen the billowing dust as the excavator knocked down walls. Suddenly, he needed to pee. We went to find a bathroom. As were driving, the Grubhub driver called. "I can't get into the building." I pulled over on the roadside, let out Ro so he could pee, stood so I was shielding him, and called D to let him know. D's phone was glitchy. I finally yelled, "There's a delivery outside for you," just as Ro finished peeing. "Oh," D finally said, "We already got that." I asked him to call us back. Maybe we'd get a better connection. He did. We sang "Happy Birthday" and chatted about his various gourmet smoothies as he tried them. Ro interrupted. "Did my tooth fall out?!" I looked. His tooth was missing. Oh no. I tell D and N goodbye. Ro starts crying: "I've been waiting so long! I've been so excited! Now the Tooth Fairy will never come." It was the donut. The tooth must have fallen into the donut. And Ro swallowed it. This means the tooth is not lost, exactly. Ro doesn't find this news comforting. (Later, K and I will offer to sift through Ro's poop. "No thanks.") As Ro cries, I let him know him the Tooth Fairy will absolutely accept a small stone as a replacement tooth. "I'll never get my real tooth," he says. "I can't put it on the family altar." That's true. We are sad. Ro continues crying. I call and tell K. She cries. I take Ro to Wendy's for a burger and fries, which he says helps him feel "a little less sad." When we get home, he searches through the pebbles in our driveway for a replacement tooth. He chooses one that sparkles in the sunlight.

August 22, 2021

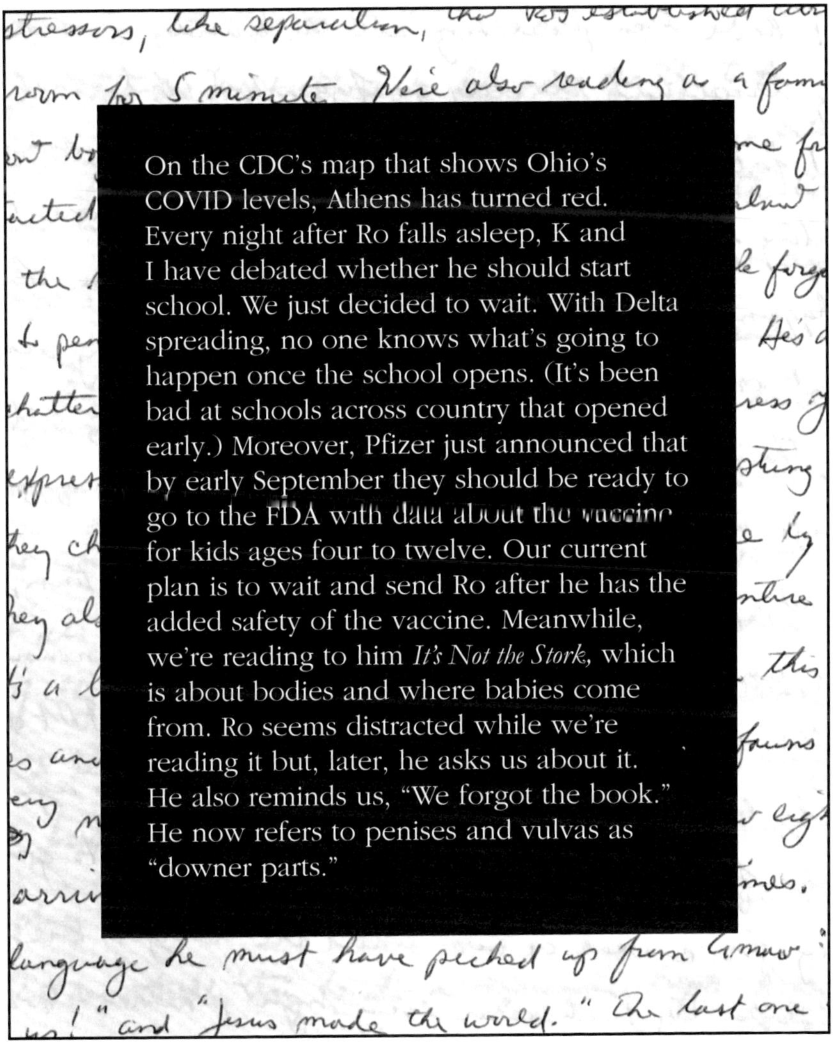

On the CDC's map that shows Ohio's COVID levels, Athens has turned red. Every night after Ro falls asleep, K and I have debated whether he should start school. We just decided to wait. With Delta spreading, no one knows what's going to happen once the school opens. (It's been bad at schools across country that opened early.) Moreover, Pfizer just announced that by early September they should be ready to go to the FDA with data about the vaccine for kids ages four to twelve. Our current plan is to wait and send Ro after he has the added safety of the vaccine. Meanwhile, we're reading to him *It's Not the Stork,* which is about bodies and where babies come from. Ro seems distracted while we're reading it but, later, he asks us about it. He also reminds us, "We forgot the book." He now refers to penises and vulvas as "downer parts."

how he called out, again and again

August 29, 2021

The Delta variant has reached Athens. As I write, our active case count is at 365. Most of these are in people under twenty-nine. Athens Public Schools stayed open for two days before shutting down because of an outbreak among school bus drivers. I felt full of dread when I went into campus to teach on the first day. One of my classes has thirty-five students and takes place in a windowless basement. Among the many stressors, Ro is now actively disliking *It's Not the Stork*. We got to how babies are made, and he decided he would pretend not to listen and draw in his notebook instead. His responses bubble up later. He's repeatedly asked K what about the book she finds the most interesting. When she asks him the same question, he doesn't answer. He did say, "I'm not getting married" and "I'm not going to have a family." He also said, "Mama, I'm sure a lot of kids feel this way, but I just want to know everything before everyone else. I feel a bit ashamed to admit it, but I am sure a lot of other kids feel that way too. It's kind of a kid feeling." If only non-kids were so self-aware. Speaking of, Grampy Roo is now sending us blog posts that refer to the "vaccine" in quotation marks. We learned that he and Grammy Roo are

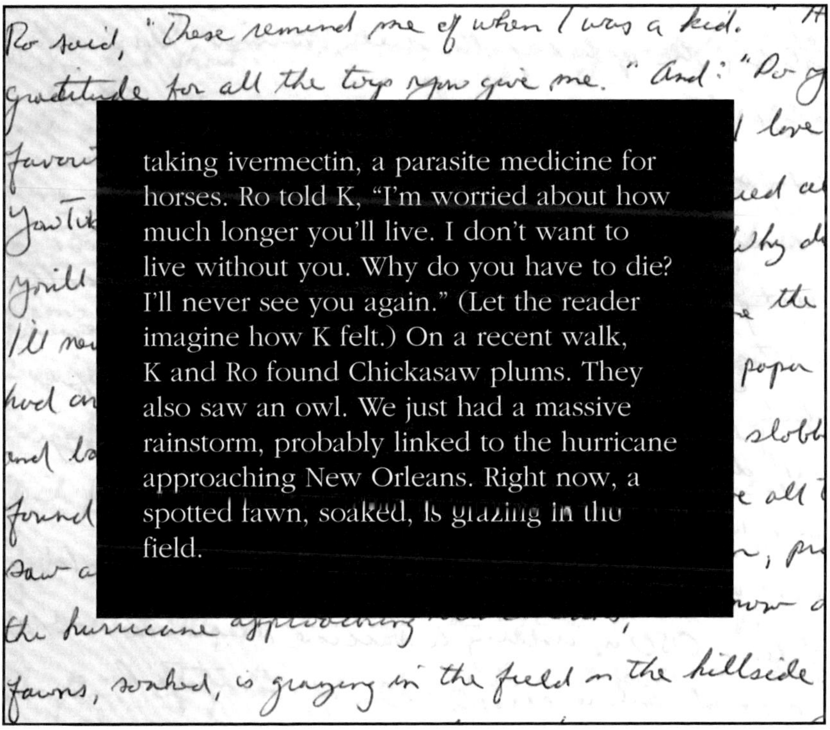

taking ivermectin, a parasite medicine for horses. Ro told K, "I'm worried about how much longer you'll live. I don't want to live without you. Why do you have to die? I'll never see you again." (Let the reader imagine how K felt.) On a recent walk, K and Ro found Chickasaw plums. They also saw an owl. We just had a massive rainstorm, probably linked to the hurricane approaching New Orleans. Right now, a spotted fawn, soaked, is grazing in the field.

I can't breathe.

September 5, 2021

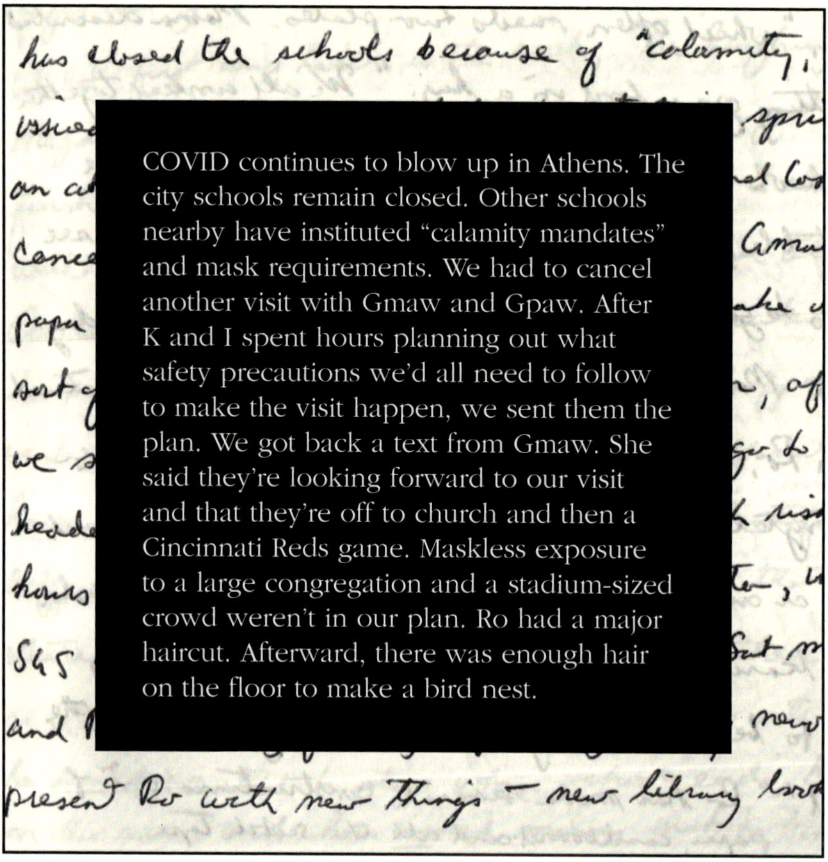

COVID continues to blow up in Athens. The city schools remain closed. Other schools nearby have instituted "calamity mandates" and mask requirements. We had to cancel another visit with Gmaw and Gpaw. After K and I spent hours planning out what safety precautions we'd all need to follow to make the visit happen, we sent them the plan. We got back a text from Gmaw. She said they're looking forward to our visit and that they're off to church and then a Cincinnati Reds game. Maskless exposure to a large congregation and a stadium-sized crowd weren't in our plan. Ro had a major haircut. Afterward, there was enough hair on the floor to make a bird nest.

September 12, 2021

Since we don't know when/if Ro will go to his actual school, we started an at-home, ad hoc alternative. For literacy, Ro made up his own story: "Once upon a time, there was a baddie. He got into the mobile jail. He pushed the button. He put dynamite on his car to free the other baddie. 'Now can I put on my hat?' 'Okay, okay, you can put it on, but just don't eat all of my peanut butter and jelly sandwiches!'" He drew a picture of a police badge to go with it. He also came up with the best name for a burger joint: "Hamburger Attack!" We're also listening to stories from around the world on the podcast *Circle Round.* As we do, we color the illustrations that go with them. If the stories get even slightly intense, Ro leaves the room and listens to them from downstairs. For science, Ro and K went off searching for seeds and found twenty different kinds between our house and the bench on the hilltop. They also identified four different kinds of acorns. Ro is keeping a nature journal and likes it so much that, when microschool ends, he goes off to journal on his own. He's asked K not to "interrupt" him. Today, we emptied the pool. Ro decided to skinny dip. He also saved a worm that was wriggling in a puddle of drained water. "I

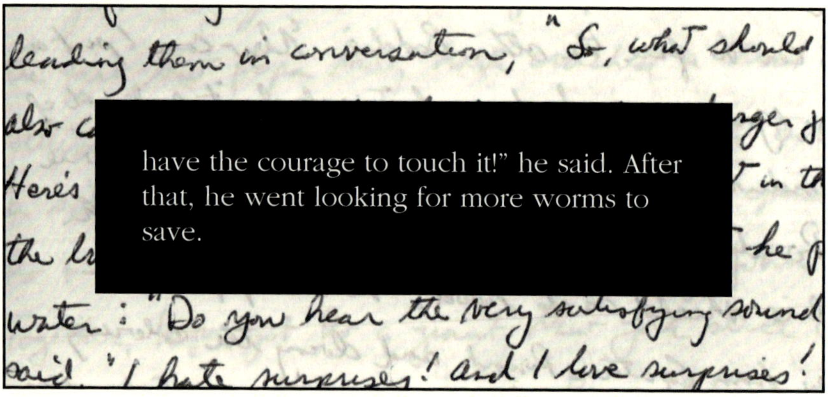
leading them in conversation, "So, what should

have the courage to touch it!" he said. After that, he went looking for more worms to save.

water: "Do you hear the very satisfying sound

said. "I hate surprises! and I love surprises!

I remember goldfinches, springing

September 19, 2021

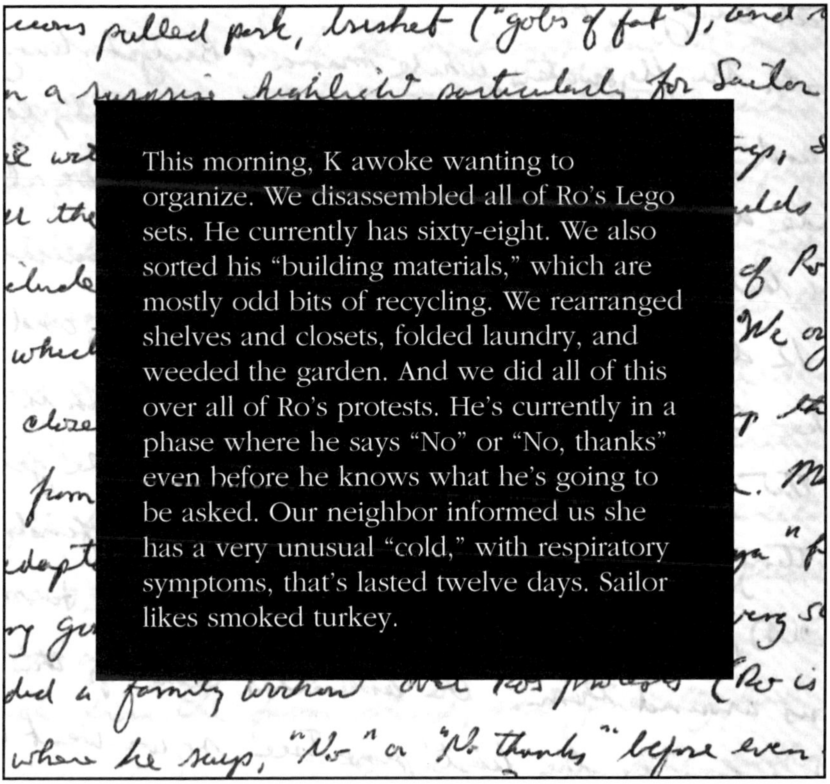

This morning, K awoke wanting to organize. We disassembled all of Ro's Lego sets. He currently has sixty-eight. We also sorted his "building materials," which are mostly odd bits of recycling. We rearranged shelves and closets, folded laundry, and weeded the garden. And we did all of this over all of Ro's protests. He's currently in a phase where he says "No" or "No, thanks" even before he knows what he's going to be asked. Our neighbor informed us she has a very unusual "cold," with respiratory symptoms, that's lasted twelve days. Sailor likes smoked turkey.

from the high grass like laughter.

September 26, 2021

Ro has become a fan of skateboarder, snowboarder, and Olympic gold-medalist Shaun White. Shaun made an appearance on *Blippi,* currently one of Ro's favorite shows, so we now talk all about Shaun White. Where is he? What's he doing? How do we find the specific T-shirt he gave to Blippi? Ro and I had a playdate with one of the kids from his school. We built a puppet theater. We also made "ghosts" by lighting empty teabags on fire and watching them float in the air.

October 3, 2021

A few minutes ago, as Ro and I were pulling out of the parking lot by the skate park, Ro said, "Look! Caves!" "What's that?" I said. "Caves," he said. "Where?" He pointed down the street to the sign in front of CVS. Ah, yes: C[a]V[e]S. Earlier in the week, Ro had a tough encounter while he was skating. I was holding his hands so he could practice popping up on his rear wheels, when two older girls sitting nearby apparently said, "He's not very good." I didn't hear them, but Ro did. He brought it up later that night. "Did you hear those orange girls say, 'He's not very good'?" (The girls were wearing matching orange soccer uniforms.) We talked about how that wasn't nice and how the orange girls also hadn't seen all the cool moves he can do. Today, back at the park, he said, "I'll show you where the orange girls were." He took me to the picnic table where they were sitting. We also went to Libby's pumpkin patch. Ro rode the "sack" slide, the toy tractor, and the real tractor. He also climbed on top of a giant caterpillar made of haystacks. Finally, we each picked out one pumpkin. Somehow, by the time I went to pay for them, Ro and K had added seven more pumpkins to our cart.

I remember you asking to play

October 10, 2021

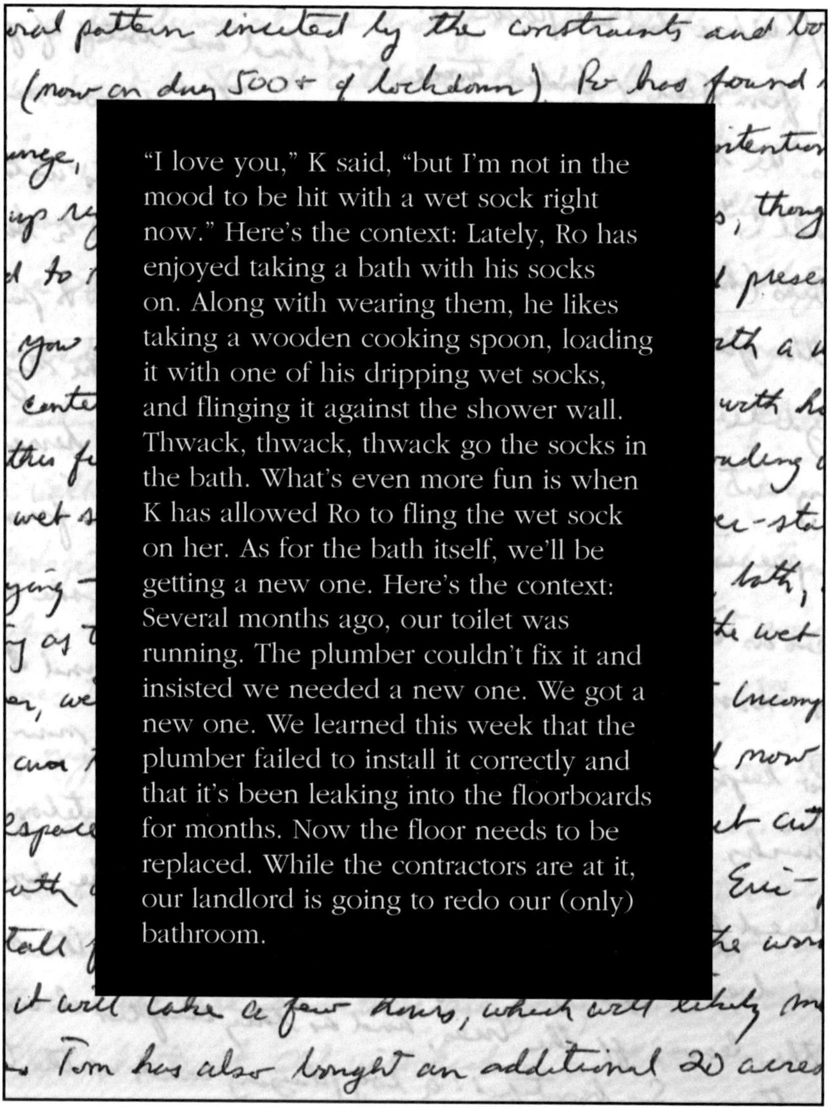

"I love you," K said, "but I'm not in the mood to be hit with a wet sock right now." Here's the context: Lately, Ro has enjoyed taking a bath with his socks on. Along with wearing them, he likes taking a wooden cooking spoon, loading it with one of his dripping wet socks, and flinging it against the shower wall. Thwack, thwack, thwack go the socks in the bath. What's even more fun is when K has allowed Ro to fling the wet sock on her. As for the bath itself, we'll be getting a new one. Here's the context: Several months ago, our toilet was running. The plumber couldn't fix it and insisted we needed a new one. We got a new one. We learned this week that the plumber failed to install it correctly and that it's been leaking into the floorboards for months. Now the floor needs to be replaced. While the contractors are at it, our landlord is going to redo our (only) bathroom.

in the bedroom, always *in the bedroom*

October 17, 2021

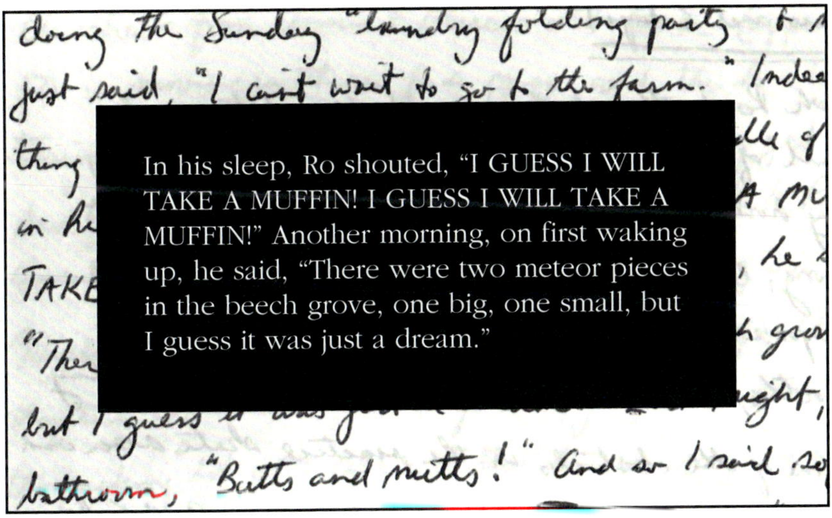

In his sleep, Ro shouted, "I GUESS I WILL TAKE A MUFFIN! I GUESS I WILL TAKE A MUFFIN!" Another morning, on first waking up, he said, "There were two meteor pieces in the beech grove, one big, one small, but I guess it was just a dream."

October 24, 2021

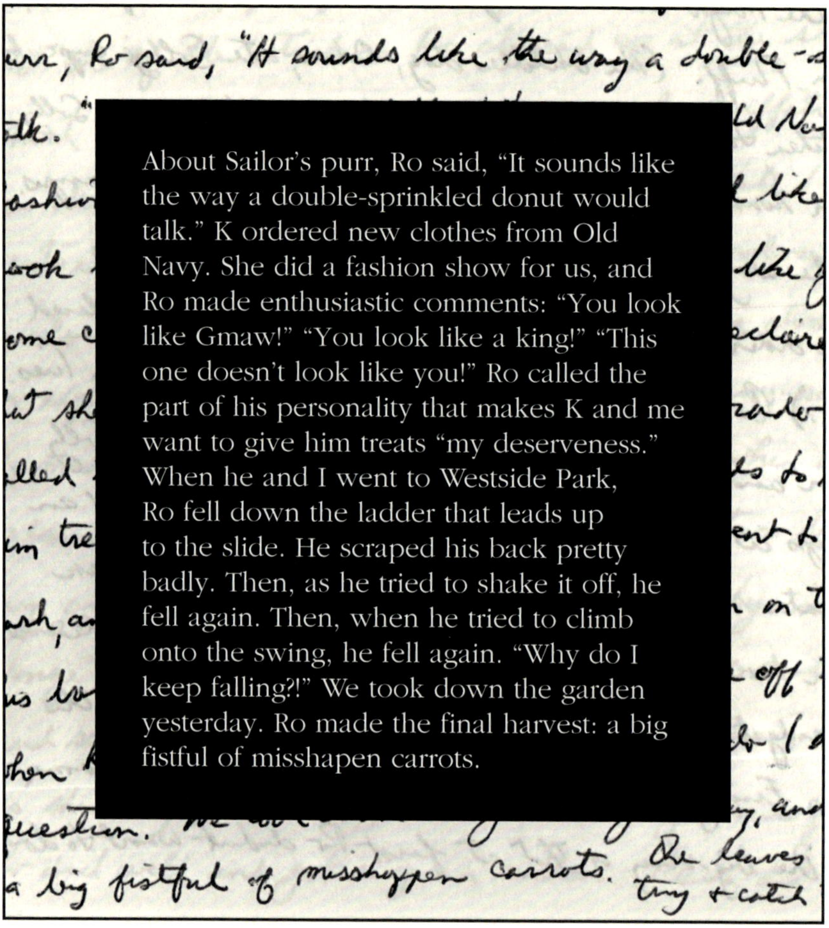
About Sailor's purr, Ro said, "It sounds like the way a double-sprinkled donut would talk." K ordered new clothes from Old Navy. She did a fashion show for us, and Ro made enthusiastic comments: "You look like Gmaw!" "You look like a king!" "This one doesn't look like you!" Ro called the part of his personality that makes K and me want to give him treats "my deserveness." When he and I went to Westside Park, Ro fell down the ladder that leads up to the slide. He scraped his back pretty badly. Then, as he tried to shake it off, he fell again. Then, when he tried to climb onto the swing, he fell again. "Why do I keep falling?!" We took down the garden yesterday. Ro made the final harvest: a big fistful of misshapen carrots.

into a slide, a fort, a tower, a truck

October 31, 2021

Ro awoke at 5:00 am, a long time to wait until "seven, oh, oh," even when it's not Halloween. At 7:00 am, he finally got to get up and find his jack-o'-lantern, stuffed with Blow Pops and three flip books featuring Charlie Chaplin. He's been in his Charlie outfit all morning. We went to P's house to celebrate. Ro and P played their ritual game of golf, but this time Ro-as-Charlie used his cane as a golf club. Earlier in the week, Ro got a new shovel as part of K's plan to plant fifty perennials in our yard. Currently, there's an outbreak of muddy divots around the house, including a giant muddy hole under the storm drain. Ro dug it "so the water could flow better."

how we spent hours there

November 7, 2021

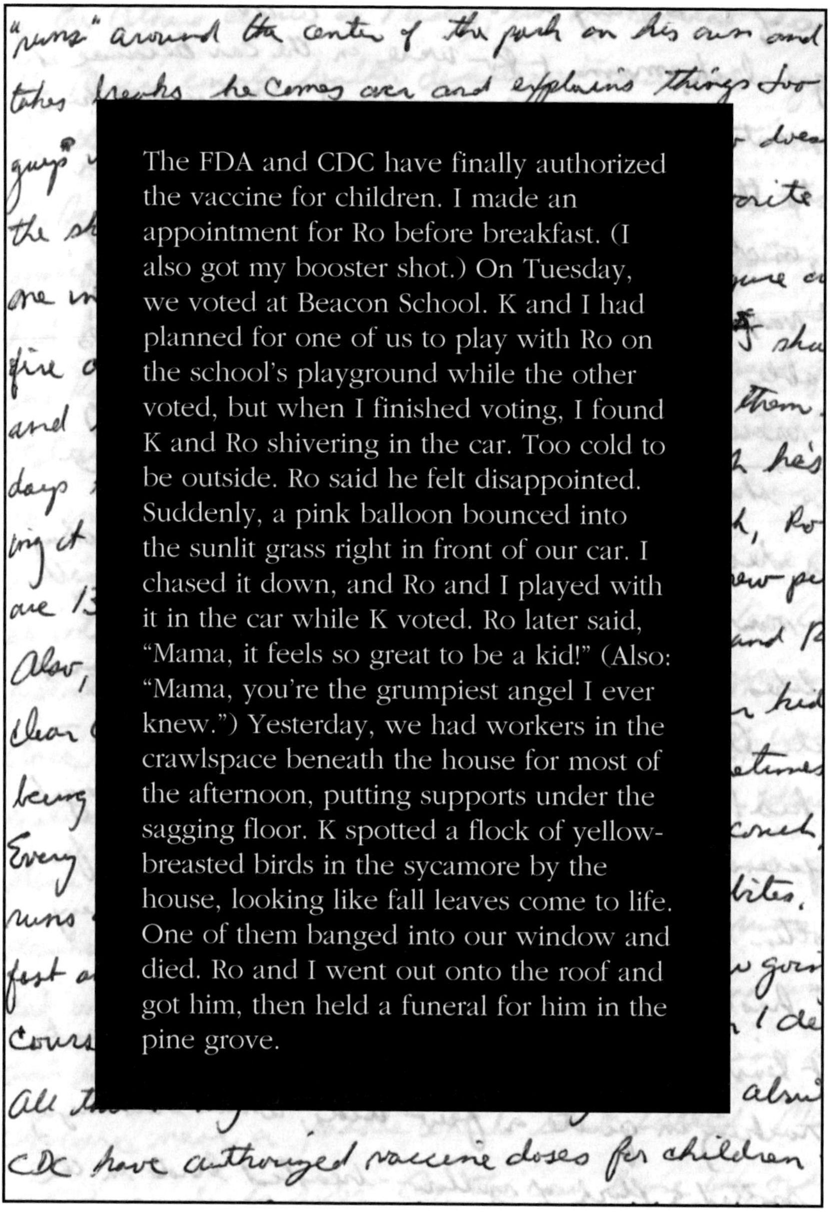

The FDA and CDC have finally authorized the vaccine for children. I made an appointment for Ro before breakfast. (I also got my booster shot.) On Tuesday, we voted at Beacon School. K and I had planned for one of us to play with Ro on the school's playground while the other voted, but when I finished voting, I found K and Ro shivering in the car. Too cold to be outside. Ro said he felt disappointed. Suddenly, a pink balloon bounced into the sunlit grass right in front of our car. I chased it down, and Ro and I played with it in the car while K voted. Ro later said, "Mama, it feels so great to be a kid!" (Also: "Mama, you're the grumpiest angel I ever knew.") Yesterday, we had workers in the crawlspace beneath the house for most of the afternoon, putting supports under the sagging floor. K spotted a flock of yellow-breasted birds in the sycamore by the house, looking like fall leaves come to life. One of them banged into our window and died. Ro and I went out onto the roof and got him, then held a funeral for him in the pine grove.

your shrieks ricocheting off the walls.

November 14, 2021

Ro got vaccinated! We'd planned to wait for the clinic in Athens, but I found an open slot at the Meiggs County Health Department in Pomeroy. When we told Ro, he said, "I'm just so excited for my big day!" On the way there, he added he was "a little nervous." When we arrived, we had to wait a while, so we played a few rounds of Who Am I? Then it was Ro's turn for the shot. He chose his right arm. He winced, and that was it. Then he had a choice: matchbox car or coloring book? He deliberated, then chose the coloring book, then instantly forgot about it, because it was time for ice cream. On Yelp, K had looked up "Best Ice Cream in Pomeroy" and found a place called McClure's, which may be the only place for ice cream in Pomeroy, given the length of the line at the drive-thru. And McClure's didn't have sprinkles. We took our sprinkle-less ice cream to a park that runs along the Ohio River, sat in a gazebo, and watched the brown and murky water flow by. On the far side of the river, trains whistled. We saw a paddlewheel boat called the *Mudstock* and wondered if it took people on rides. The next day, Ro had a sore arm and felt droopy. "I feel like I don't work anymore," he said. This morning, the first snow of the

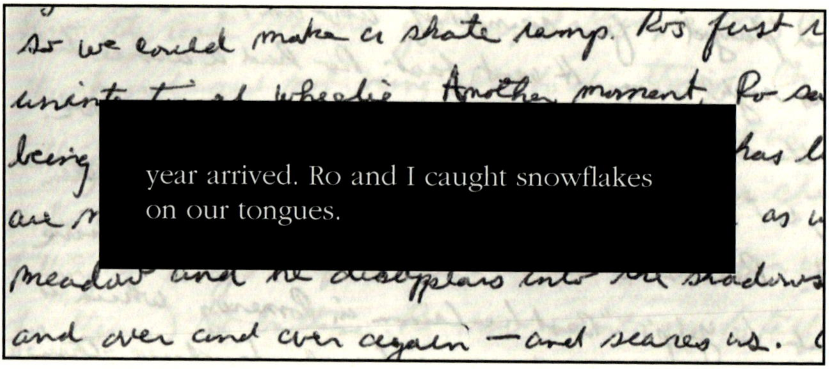

year arrived. Ro and I caught snowflakes on our tongues.

November 21, 2021

Ro and I did a grocery run into town to pick up, among other Thanksgiving items, a massive fifteen-pound turkey that K had ordered. As soon as I saw it, I looked at Ro and said, "Mama is going to freak out." When we got home, K freaked out. ("How should we store it? What will it do to the internal temperature of the fridge? Will the air in the fridge still circulate properly with it in there?") That night, I had secondary stress dreams about the turkey. Thanksgiving, here we come. A giant beach tree fell down the hillside near Margaret's Creek. Ro decided to climb it, starting at what once were its highest branches and making his way along its trunk to its unearthed roots. Its bark is rough and gray and wrinkly, like an elephant's hide.

I remember how these days disappeared

November 27, 2021

Before Thanksgiving Day, there was "Pie Day." First, K and Ro made pumpkin pie. Then Ro and I made a pirate hat out of construction paper, with Ro stressing the *pie* in *pirate*. We also did a pirate puzzle while listening to pirate shanties. And we read a book called *Pie Rats*. At the end of the day, we picked up more pie from town. (Ro stated definitively that his favorite pie is cherry.) Thanksgiving arrived the next day, at 6:50 am. Ro awoke, all energy. We feasted with eggs, bacon, and babka. Then it was time to cook the turkey. We cleared the kitchen in case any bacteria-laden turkey juice were to splatter. K removed the giblets. I did a quick YouTube study of how to butcher a turkey and learned I needed to yank the turkey's joints out of their sockets. Into the oven went the turkey. We took a break and walked down to the creek, where we played a game of Poohsticks. We used massive logs, which made for much better splashes. Then we returned to the house for one of K's innovations: Thanksgiving presents. Ro opened a Lego skate park and built it as K prepared our feast of turkey, mashed potatoes and gravy, creamed greens, rice pilaf, stuffing, beet salad, roasted vegetables, and rolls. After we ate, Ro and I groaned and pretended our pants had exploded. Then pie. We gave Ro the can of whipped cream and let him try to shoot it into our mouths. He mostly missed. The next day, he woke up again at 6:50 am. "Time to get the Christmas tree!" K started singing Christmas carols, belting "Joy to the World" and cackling hysterically. Ro unboxed our mechanical singing snowman. He hit the play button over and over. And over. At White's Mill, we were the first ones. Ro fell in love with every tree. K fell in love with every large tree. By the end of the day, our medium-sized tree was set up, our lights were strung inside and out, and our Christmas decorations covered the house. Ro looked exhausted.

and how I wished you knew

December 5, 2021

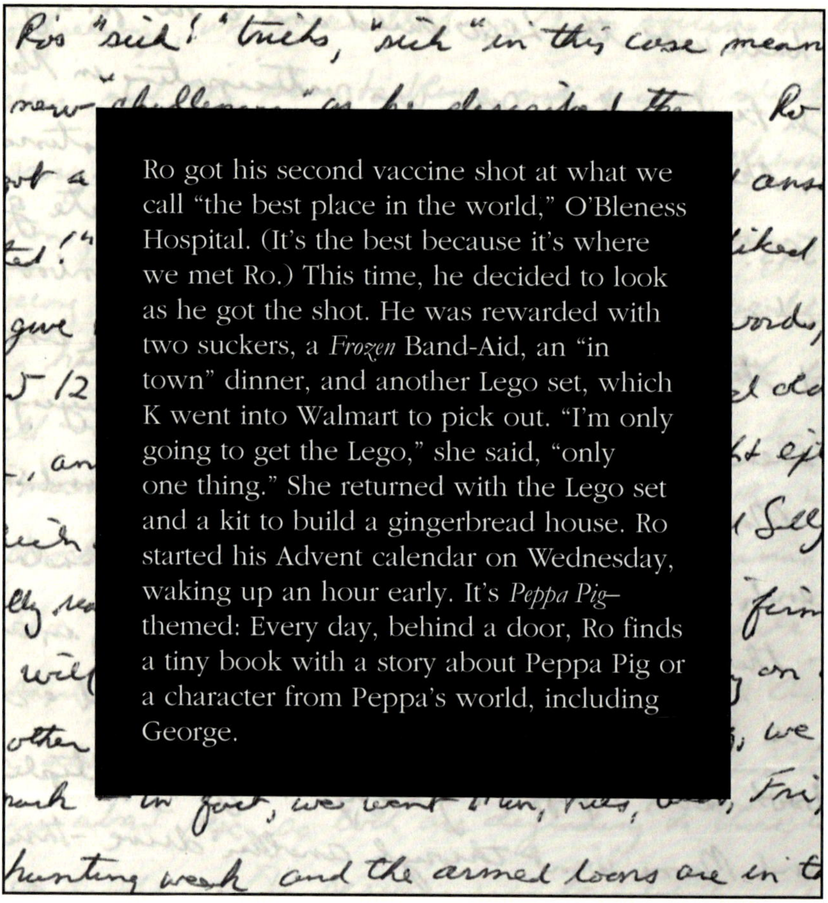

Ro got his second vaccine shot at what we call "the best place in the world," O'Bleness Hospital. (It's the best because it's where we met Ro.) This time, he decided to look as he got the shot. He was rewarded with two suckers, a *Frozen* Band-Aid, an "in town" dinner, and another Lego set, which K went into Walmart to pick out. "I'm only going to get the Lego," she said, "only one thing." She returned with the Lego set and a kit to build a gingerbread house. Ro started his Advent calendar on Wednesday, waking up an hour early. It's *Peppa Pig*–themed: Every day, behind a door, Ro finds a tiny book with a story about Peppa Pig or a character from Peppa's world, including George.

December 13, 2021

On Sunday, we all went to Ro's school, where the school board was meeting. (K is now secretary.) Ro and I played outside with some of his friends. Afterward, I made the last-minute decision to take Ro to a memorial ceremony that the board was holding. One of the board's founding members had recently died of cancer. (I thought this would be Ro's first chance to attend a funeral, but now, as I write, I remember he was at Grandma Mary's funeral when he was one, so this will be the first funeral Ro will remember.) We met behind the school, where a new bench had been built. It had a plaque with the man's name on it. Next to it was a newly planted sapling, a white oak, which is a species that lives hundreds of years and grows a special kind of acorn that people can eat. White oaks are also "mother trees" that take care of the other trees near them. We heard all this from one of the man's friends, who likened him to a white oak. He then asked his daughter to sprinkle some of the man's ashes in a ring around the tree's roots, where they'd be absorbed by the tree. Afterward, each of us took turns shoveling compost over the ashes, so they'd stay there and feed the tree. As we did, we formed a second ring around the oak, and each of us said a few words about the man. That was it. Ro wasn't sure what to make of the ritual stillness. At one point, he asked one of the other kids if she wanted to go play. K went over to quiet him, and he threw a little tantrum, which I'd never seen him do. Eventually, he settled. Later, he let us know he found it "boring" but "strange too." I love that as he grows up and the tree grow up, he'll see this memorial every day he's at school. Death growing into life, life growing out of death. After the ceremony, Ro and the other kids got extremely muddy digging a trench in a (different) compost pile.

for me to love you.

December 19, 2021

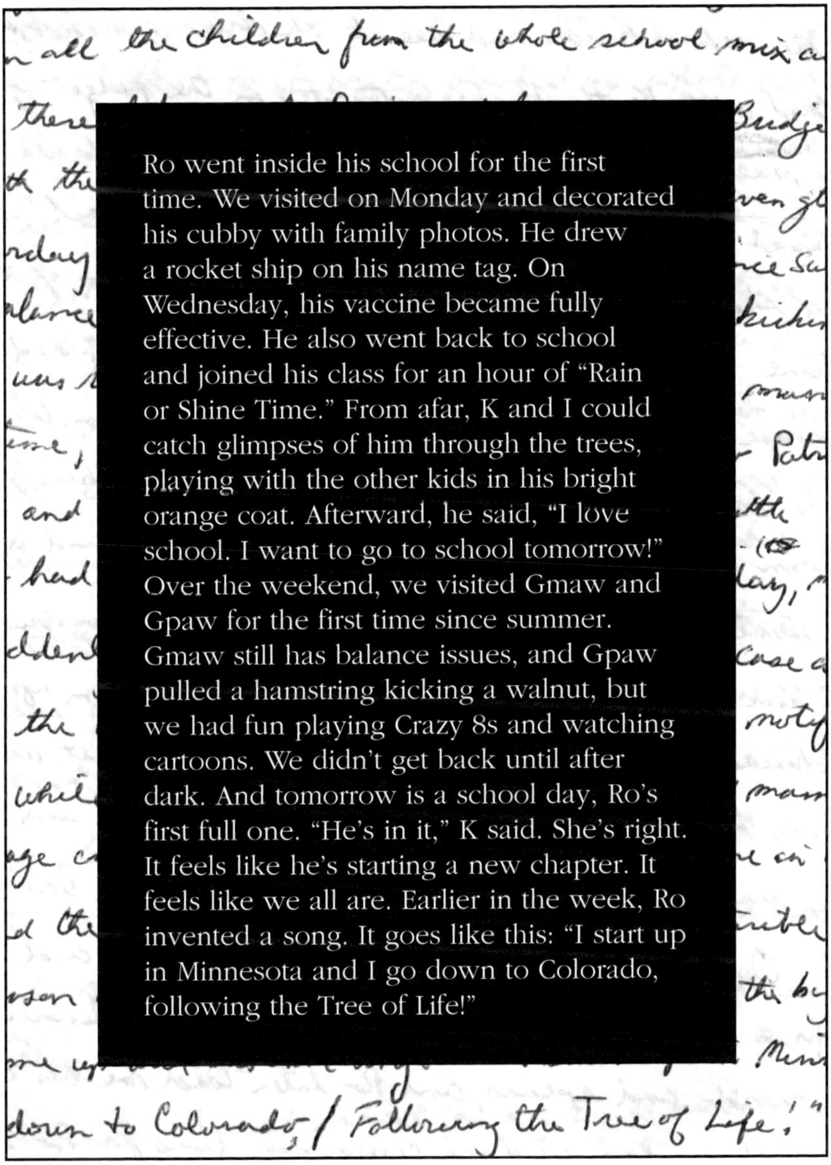

Ro went inside his school for the first time. We visited on Monday and decorated his cubby with family photos. He drew a rocket ship on his name tag. On Wednesday, his vaccine became fully effective. He also went back to school and joined his class for an hour of "Rain or Shine Time." From afar, K and I could catch glimpses of him through the trees, playing with the other kids in his bright orange coat. Afterward, he said, "I love school. I want to go to school tomorrow!" Over the weekend, we visited Gmaw and Gpaw for the first time since summer. Gmaw still has balance issues, and Gpaw pulled a hamstring kicking a walnut, but we had fun playing Crazy 8s and watching cartoons. We didn't get back until after dark. And tomorrow is a school day, Ro's first full one. "He's in it," K said. She's right. It feels like he's starting a new chapter. It feels like we all are. Earlier in the week, Ro invented a song. It goes like this: "I start up in Minnesota and I go down to Colorado, following the Tree of Life!"

*

"Taste Test!"

I am heading up the stairs, carrying a tray with three tubs of sherbet and as many spoons. In a week, on International Transgender Day of Visibility, I will tell the world I'm nonbinary—the world, in this case, being my 658 followers on Twitter—but right now I'm about to tell the person I love most. He's six. He loves taste tests.

"Really?" he asks, eyeing the tubs.

"Yep," I say, setting down the tray on a battered trunk we use as a table. I line up the spoons. He grins.

I didn't figure out I was nonbinary until I was fifty-one, about the same time I started hearing from the AARP. At first, I felt an existential vertigo, realizing I'd lived roughly half a century estranged from my true self. Yet, I also felt a delight, even a lightness, in finally being more me. I wanted to share that with my son.

But nonbinary, as a concept, isn't easy to explain. I don't entirely get it, and I *am* it. How would I explain it to a six-year-old?

So, buddy, there's this thing called *the gender binary*. It's why you call me "Papa" and Mama "Mama," and you've been living in it since the moment you were born. But here's the thing, buddy, the gender binary isn't real. Sure, some people are men, and some are women, but that doesn't mean that there are only two genders. Gender is vast. It's varied. Some people don't fit into these categories. They're called *nonbinary*. Now, as a term, *nonbinary* actively negates the violent division of humanity into two socially constructed biopolitical categories that uphold the West's white-hetero-patriarchal-colonial-capitalist project and, in doing so, carves out a liberatory space for heretofore unnamed and perhaps unimagined genders. And that, buddy, is me.

In the end, I decided I needed something a little more child-friendly than queer theory. I went with sherbet.

I intended to serve my son blueberry, raspberry, and rainbow sherbet to represent different genders: male, female, and all the fruity rest of us. Then he and I would eat our way beyond the binary. I thought this explanation would be playful and sweet, while also saving my son from a theoretical brain-freeze. Plus, rainbow sherbet has the pride flag swirled right into it.

However, when I started poking around the giant freezers at Kroger, I couldn't find any blueberry, and the store was inexplicably out of rainbow sherbet. I ended up getting mango for male and for nonbinary I had to settle on a frighteningly vibrant flavor called "Tie-Dye Burst."

Nonetheless, I pressed on and brought home my metaphors.

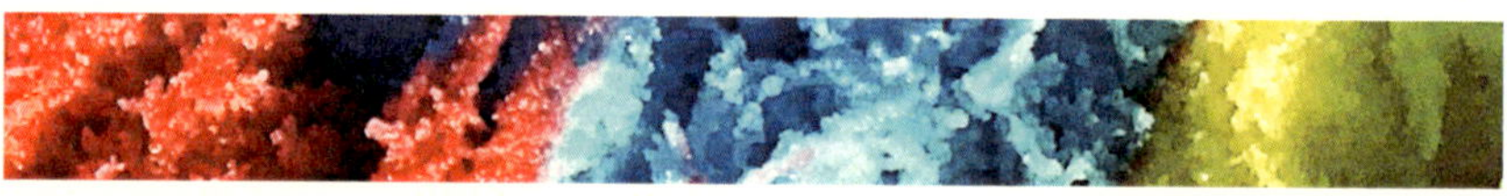

"You know how some people are female, like Mama?" I ask.

We're at the trunk. Mama is with us. We each have a spoon.

"Yes," my son says.

"They're sort of like this raspberry." I peel back the top on the first tub and expose the ruby rich sherbet. "Let's take a bite."

We do, and my son gives it a thumbs up. That's his rating system.

"And you know how some people are male," I go on, "like Gpaw?"

"Yes," he says.

"They're sort of like this mango."

Again, I peel off the lid, and we each take a spoonful. Again, the thumbs up.

"And then there are some people who aren't raspberry or mango, like Taz." Taz is a gender-expansive kid at my son's school. I feel a rush of gratitude for this child who knows themself and whose parents know them, love them, and support them. What, I wonder, might my life have been like if, at six, I'd known who I was. What if I'd had parents who would have loved me for who I was? Like so many of us, I did not.

"Yes," says my son.

"Well, they're sort of like this." With a flourish, I pop the final top and let all of those lavishly abundant tie-dye colors burst.

My son ahs.

Another spoonful, another thumb.

"So," I say, "I'm like this sherbet. I'm not mango. I'm not a man."

My son pauses. For a long, long beat, he stares into his empty spoon.

At last, he looks up at me and says, “That’s a big thought.”

And it is, one I suddenly feel grateful he’s willing to think with me. I feel it as a rush, as a mix of sugar and relief, him seeing me, me seeing him, as we begin this bigger us.

Acknowledgments

Earlier versions of material in this book previously appeared in *Brevity, DIAGRAM, Essay Daily, River Teeth, Terrain, Territory,* and a limited-edition chapbook published by *Cutbank,* the literary journal of the University of Montana. My thanks to the editors of these publications for their support and to the editorial team at Kent State University Press for publishing this book.

My thanks also to the Ohio Arts Council for a grant that supported the writing of this book and to Ohio University for support in the publication of it.

The materials under erasure in "Remember Me" are from my medical records for cancer treatment. The quotes and paraphrases of Itaru Sasaki's words in "Text Our Dead" come from Tessa Fontaine's "The Phone of the Wind," published in *The Believer.*

This is a book that might not have been. Unlike others, I've had the luck to live. I am grateful for this life and, above all, for the chance to share it with Roland LeMay.